D0910341

Fishing
Maryland, Delaware, and Washington, D.C.

Help Us Keep This Guide Up to Date

Every effort has been made by the authors and editors to make this guide as accurate and useful as possible. However, many things can change after a guide is published—trails are rerouted, regulations change, techniques evolve, facilities come under new management, and so forth.

We welcome your comments concerning your experiences with this guide and how you feel it could be improved and kept up to date. While we may not be able to respond to all comments and suggestions, we'll take them to heart, and we'll also make certain to share them with the authors. Please send your comments and suggestions to the following address:

The Globe Pequot Press
Reader Response/Editorial Department
P.O. Box 480
Guilford, CT 06437

Or you may e-mail us at:

editorial@GlobePequot.com

Thanks for your input, and happy angling!

Fishing
Maryland, Delaware, and Washington, D.C.

An Angler's Guide to More Than 100
Fresh and Saltwater Fishing Spots

MARTIN FREED AND
RUTA VASKYS

THE LYONS PRESS
GUILFORD, CONNECTICUT
AN IMPRINT OF THE GLOBE PEQUOT PRESS

To buy books in quantity for corporate use
or incentives, call **(800) 962–0973**
or e-mail **premiums@GlobePequot.com**.

The Lyons Press is an imprint of The Globe Pequot Press.

Text design by Casey Shain
Photos by Martin Freed and Ruta Vaskys
Maps created by Ryan Mitchell © Morris Book Publishing, LLC

Library of Congress Cataloging-in-Publication data is available on file.
ISBN 978-0-7627-4445-9

Printed in the United States of America
10 9 8 7 6 5 4 3 2 1

This book is dedicated to all people who enjoy the great outdoors, especially those who actively work to preserve this great resource for future generations.

Also to Martin's uncle Ed Stern, who was responsible for turning him into a fishing nut; and to Ruta's parents, who took her fishing every week on the Severn River in Crownsville.

Contents

Overview

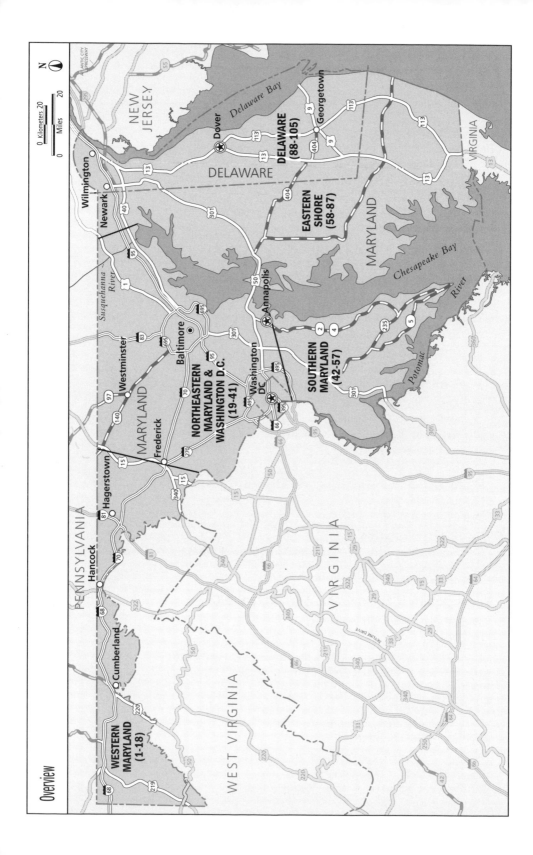

Acknowledgments

While much of the information in this book is from personal experience, a number of others have contributed.

We would like to thank all the friendly folks at the bait and tackle shops for the help we received. Also, the dedicated public servants at the Maryland Department of Natural Resources have been most helpful. Some of the locations and angling techniques are written up on their Web site as public information. The Delaware Department of Natural Resources and its Web site have also been helpful.

Introduction

Maryland, the Free State, may feel just like that to avid anglers. So many low-cost angling opportunities exist that it is highly unlikely that if you fished every day of your life, you would ever angle at every location. Delaware, the First State, is perhaps first in the minds of anglers for variety: long stretches of sandy beach, tidal rivers, and great fishing ponds. Combined, the two states are like a mini-America. They stretch from the Atlantic Ocean to the protected waters of the Chesapeake through the Piedmont to the mountains in the west.

Co-author Ruta Vaskys hoists a hefty black drum caught near Deal Island.

Like the terrain, the fishing is diverse. From marlin in the offshore waters to fighting rockfish in the Chesapeake, to oversize largemouths in the ponds and lakes to trophy trout in the mountain rivers, what more can a dedicated angler ask for?

In this book we give a sampling of what an angler can expect from the two states and Washington, D.C. Though more than a hundred locations are described, they represent just a small number of the total.

We wrote this book after a lifetime of fishing, and hope the reader will enjoy as many hours as we have in pursuit of this sport.

Hazards and Precautions

Snakes

Though the overwhelming majority of snakes in Maryland and Delaware are harmless and a vital part of the environment, a few species of poisonous ones are present. While snakebites are rare, anyone venturing into the wilderness should take certain precautions.

Not all snakebites can be prevented, but a few simple steps will greatly reduce the risk:

- Know how to identify poisonous and non-venomous species.
- Take a snakebite kit and become familiar with its use.
- Know where to go for help.
- Know the most common symptoms of snakebite:
    a) bloody discharge at the wound site
    b) fang marks
    c) swelling at the site of the bite
    d) severe localized pain and discoloration
    e) swollen lymph nodes near the bite
    f) diarrhea, burning, convulsions, fainting, and/or dizziness

The symptoms may resemble other medical conditions. Consult a physician if you think you've been bitten.

Treatment for snakebites: Stay calm and act quickly. Get help fast, but while waiting for assistance, do the following:

1. Wash the bite with soap and water.
2. Keep the bitten area lower than the heart.
3. Apply a cool compress.
4. Monitor breathing and heart rate.
5. Remove all rings, watches, and constrictive clothing, in case of swelling.

If unable to get help within thirty minutes, the American Red Cross recommends the following:
- Apply a bandage, wrapped 2 to 4 inches above the bite, to help slow the venom. This should not cut off the flow of blood from a vein or artery—the band should be loose enough to slip a finger under it.
- A suction device can be placed over the bite to help draw venom out of the wound without making cuts. These devices are often included in commercial snakebite kits.

The best way to prevent being bitten by a snake is to avoid snakes in the first place. Follow these guidelines to stay safe:

- Do not harass any snake (or other wildlife for that matter). Many bites occur as a result of someone trying to kill a snake or get too close to it.
- Do not walk through tall grass unless absolutely necessary. Stick to the hiking paths as much as possible.
- Watch where you put your hands and feet.
- Be especially cautious when scrambling among rocks.

Most important, do not let a fear of snakes stop you from having a good time in the outdoors. Bites are very rare. Just take some precautions.

Insects and Arachnids
These critters are more annoying and some say as dangerous as snakes. However, just a few simple precautions can save the day.

Mosquitoes: These are the most common pests. In some areas, especially the low-lands, they could carry diseases, some that are life threatening. However, they are easily deterred:

- Use a repellent. Many think that the most effective are products that contain deet. The higher the percentage of this ingredient, the better. If you do not want to use deet, Natrapel does work but perhaps not as well.
- Mosquitoes are most active around dusk. Staying indoors during this time will limit exposure.
- Wear clothes covering most of your skin.
- Some people also wear head nets.

No-see-ums, or gnats: If you ever had to spend a night dealing with these guys, it will be long remembered. Some call them sand fleas, as they are usually found in sandy or gravelly areas. They are small enough to pass through all but the finest screens. Make sure your tent or camper is so outfitted.

Surfcasting on ocean beaches is a great way to spend a day.

Deet works well, and we have spread it on our screens with some success. Since these insects are attracted to light, it is best to do your reading before dark.

Ticks: Various species of ticks are found throughout Maryland and Delaware. A bite from an infected tick can result in a serious disease. Here are a few precautions:

- These guys hang on foliage waiting for a host to walk by. Stay on rocky or sandy trails.
- Rub insect repellent on your legs.
- Wear your pants inside your socks and put repellent on them. White socks are best because the ticks will be easier to spot.
- Check your skin for ticks every evening, or have your partner do it for you.
- If you happen to get a tick bite, keep in mind that the longer the critter is attached, the more likely it is to pass a disease on to you. If you can't get to medical help quickly, take a good pair of tweezers, grab your skin below the tick's mouth, and pull it off. Dab with alcohol and bandage.

Spiders: A few species of poisonous spiders inhabit Maryland and Delaware, but very few spider bites are reported. Folks usually get bit when they roll over onto the critter or try to scratch as it is walking up their body. Stay aware of what is happening around and on you.

Bears

The black-bear population is increasing in Maryland, but very few are found in Delaware. These guys are rather shy, and you should consider yourself lucky if you see one. However, a few precautions should be taken, not so much to protect humans from bears, but the other way around. It's usually the carelessness of humans that produces a nuisance animal, and occasionally one has to be dispatched.

• Always keep your food in bear-proof containers.
• Keep your campsite clean and neat.
• Do not throw garbage out into open receptacles. We've noticed that some areas in the western part of Maryland now have bear-proof garbage cans.
• Head in the opposite direction, very slowly, if a cub is seen.

Other Mammals

While raccoons, possums, foxes, coyotes, and other mammals are not usually any threat, rabies has been found in both Delaware and Maryland. This disease could make even the shyest critters aggressive. If you see any animal acting strangely, do not approach it. Move away.

Poison Ivy and Poison Oak

These plants are common in both states, and most people are at least somewhat allergic to the oils produced by their leaves. The best way to protect yourself is to learn to identify them and make sure you are not exposed. Standard clothing does not help very much. The oil can penetrate the fabric and reach your skin. In fact, you can develop the symptoms by touching the clothes after they are taken off. The oils can also be spread person to person. If one is exposed, touching someone else can give them the allergy.

In order not to ruin a trip, take an antihistamine salve along just in case someone develops the rash. A number of good ones can be bought over the counter at most pharmacies. If the condition is severe, seek medical help.

The Sun

The sun is very strong in the Mid-Atlantic states during the summer. If you are fair skinned, be sure to include a good sunscreen in your supplies. It should have an SPF of at least 25.

The best way to treat sunburn is to avoid it. However, if it happens, a number of over-the-counter remedies are available at your pharmacy. These will treat the discomfort and minimize the chances of infection. Mild cases of sunburn can be treated by taking a cool shower or applying cold cloth compresses. The application of topical agents such as aloe vera and/or salves containing hydrocortisone could be helpful.

Severe sunburn should be treated by a medical professional. Do not wait until you get home. Find a local doctor or even emergency room if necessary to take a look at the patient.

The symptoms of sun poisoning are fever, nausea, vomiting, fatigue, dizziness, red skin rash, and/or chills. Seek medical help at once.

Boating Safety

Be aware of the boating regulations and what equipment is needed. Each vessel should be equipped with one personal flotation device (PFD) for each passenger. Make sure that you have the appropriate sizes for kids and adults. Some boats require fire extinguishers, whistles, flares, and running lights. These things do get checked.

Know Your Limits

Some of the locations, especially those for wild trout, require rigorous hiking. Some of this may be downhill. That means it could be easy heading in, but you will have a more strenuous hike back up. Do not wear yourself out beyond your ability to get back to your vehicle.

Hydrilla Weed and Zebra Mussels

These two exotic organisms are very destructive to aquatic ecosystems and have done great damage to lakes and rivers where they have been accidentally introduced. They reduce fish-spawning habitat and host a number of parasites that are harmful to fish.

The following steps are recommended to prevent introduction of these pests to uncontaminated waters:

- Do not transfer bait from one body of water to another.
- Completely drain all water from your boat and trailer.
- Inspect the boat hull and engine for signs of zebra mussels and grass.
- Allow the boat and trailer to dry for at least two days before launching into an uncontaminated body of water.
- If you suspect that you've boated in contaminated waters, wash your boat and trailer with 140 degree water.
- Do not leave the boat engine in the horizontal position when in storage. This does not allow all the water to drain out of it.

Catch-and-Release Fishing

If anglers adhere to the regulations, the fisheries certainly can sustain the harvest. However, over the years catch-and-release has become more popular. In fact, in some delicate waters, it is required.

Here are a few tips for successfully releasing fish:

- One of the best things an angler can do to reduce harm to fish is to use barbless hooks. These cause a lot less damage to the fish's mouth.
- Make sure you hold the fish gently. Do not squeeze the gut area and never put your hands in the gills. Do not press on the gill area from the outside.
- Always wet your hands before handling the fish. This helps maintain the slime on the critter's body, which is required for its good health.
- Hold the fish in the stream with its head facing upstream. This will allow a flow of water over its gills and replenish the oxygen lost during the fight. Hold it there until the fish swims away on its own. You can move it back and forth to force water over its gills.
- Many anglers use hooks slightly larger than necessary for the size fish they are targeting. This reduces the number of deeply hooked fish that are caught—most will just have the hook in their lip. Needle-nose pliers will always come in handy for unhooking.

Flounder are one of the most sought-after species in saltwater.

Follow these guidelines and most released fish will whip their tails, disappear, and live to fight another day.

How to Use This Guide

This guidebook is divided into five sections: Western Maryland, Northeastern Maryland and Washington, D.C., Southern Maryland, the Eastern Shore of Maryland, and Delaware. In addition, appendixes cover trout waters in both states.

For the purposes of this book, Western Maryland is defined as the area of the state west of a line drawn north–south through Frederick. The Southern Maryland area is south of a line drawn from the southern tip of DC to Annapolis. The rest of the Western Shore and DC are included in the Northeastern Maryland section. The Eastern Shore section covers all the areas of Maryland that lie east of the Chesapeake. And Delaware is, of course, its own state.

Directions are given from either Washington, Baltimore, or Wilmington. A number followed by a letter indicates a specific access. Grid information for the appropriate DeLorme atlas and gazetteer is also included.

The waters in each chapter are very generally listed north to south. If a few are clustered, we describe them together regardless of their latitude. Most of the rivers run north–south, so we just estimate their mean latitudinal positions. If a stream or lake is located in more than one area, it is usually only listed once. A few exceptions to this rule may be found, such as the Nanticoke River, which passes through both Delaware and the Eastern Shore.

If the reader wishes to fish in a certain area, it is best to look at the map to obtain the names of some waters, then go to the table of contents to find page numbers. If you know the name of the specific water you are heading to, look it up in the index.

We do not get too involved with regulations, as they periodically change. In some cases—but definitely not all—we point out some special regulations that should be checked before fishing. It is up to the reader to keep up-to-date with the current regulations.

Only the contact names are listed in the "For more information" sections. Full contact information is included in Appendix C.

Western Maryland

Western Maryland is a land of expansive forests, babbling brooks, clear lakes, and big rivers. Fishing opportunities abound, from native brookies in small mountain streams to trophy bass in the big lakes. This section includes the counties of Garrett, Allegany, Washington, and the western parts of Frederick and Montgomery.

1 Youghiogheny River Lake (Reservoir)

Key species: Largemouth bass, smallmouth bass, chain pickerel, northern pike, walleye, crappie, channel catfish, yellow perch, bluegill and other sunfish, brown trout, rainbow trout, and carp.

Directions: From Baltimore, take the Beltway (Interstate 695) to Interstate 70 west and pick up Interstate 68 west near Hancock. Take I-68 to exit 4 (Friendsville) and go 5 miles north on Maryland Highway 53 to the US Army Corps of Engineers Mill Run Road Campground and boat ramp.

DeLorme: Maryland and Delaware Atlas & Gazetteer: Page 65 A5.

Description: Owned by the Army Corps of Engineers, the approximately 2,800-acre Youghiogheny River Reservoir is 16 miles long with 38 miles of shoreline. It has an average depth of 54 feet and a maximum depth of 121 feet. The reservoir straddles the Pennsylvania-Maryland border, starting just north of Friendsville, Maryland, and extending to the dam in Confluence, Pennsylvania. It supports a variety of fish habitats that include rocky shorelines, sunken trees and stumps, boat docks, and shallow vegetated flats that provide excellent spawning habitat.

Water fluctuations, depending on annual rainfall, are extreme, especially in the fall when it's nearly drawn down. Due to low-water levels, at times the boat ramp at the campground may not be usable, but small boats and canoes can be carried to the lake.

The fishing: Most anglers fish the Youghiogheny River Reservoir for smallmouth bass. The largemouth bass fishery is limited. Walleye fishing is good to excellent, and local fishing clubs hold open tournaments throughout the year. Trophy-size crappie and northern pike are relatively common. In addition to the key species, rock bass, brown bullhead, hybrid striped bass, and alewife are also present.

Fish populations are monitored by the Pennsylvania Fish and Boat Commission (PFBC).

Restrictions: Fishing regulations are proposed by the PFBC and summarized in the *Maryland Freshwater Sportfishing Guide.* Pennsylvania and Maryland have a cooperative agreement that allows boat anglers to fish the entire lake with either state's fishing license. Shoreline anglers must possess the appropriate license for that state.

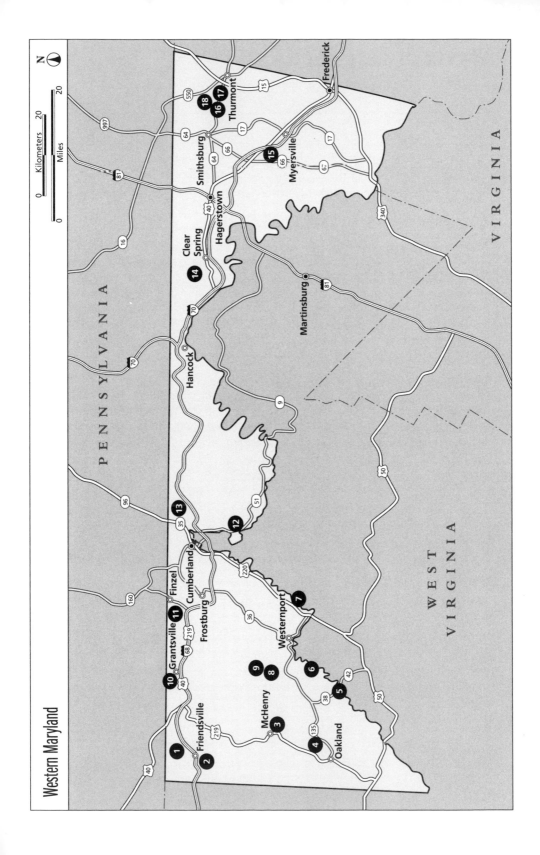

Western Maryland

Camping: The Army Corps of Engineers has a fine campground on the lake; a fee is required.

For more information: Maryland Department of Natural Resources, Fisheries Service, Western Region Office; US Army Corps of Engineers, Pittsburgh District; Garrett County Chamber of Commerce.

2 Youghiogheny River

Key species: Brown trout, rainbow trout, and smallmouth bass.

Directions: From Baltimore, take the Beltway (Interstate 695) to Interstate 70 west to Interstate 68 west. Take U.S. Highway 219 south and turn right (west) on Sang Run Road. Turn left (south) on Hoyes Run Road and continue to a stop sign. Turn right (north) on Oakland–Sang Run Road and proceed 0.1 mile to a parking area on the left side of the road just across a small bridge. A sign illustrates the access trail along the river.

DeLorme: Maryland and Delaware Atlas & Gazetteer: Page 65 C5.

Description: The Catch and Release Trophy Fishing Area (C&RTFA) is 4 miles long. It extends upstream from the Sang Run Bridge to the Deep Creek Lake Power Plant. The large river averages about 150 feet in width and has a low to moderate gradient, shallow riffles, long runs, and some deep pools. The streambed consists of cobble, boulders, and some limestone bedrock. River flow rises abruptly during dam releases, so call for scheduled release information before planning a trip.

The fishing: Both brown and rainbow trout are stocked annually. The rainbows are a warm-water strain and are able to tolerate higher temperatures than most other trout. These rainbows grow fast because of the abundant aquatic insects found in the Youghiogheny. They are silver and have very deep bodies. Brown trout grow to trophy-size, 5 pounds plus, in this river. Smallmouth bass are also common, and they put up quite a surprising fight when captured on light trout-fishing tackle.

Restrictions: Fishing in the Youghiogheny River C&RTFA is restricted to artificial lures and flies only. Please consult the *Maryland Freshwater Sportfishing Guide* for details.

For more information: Maryland Department of Natural Resources, Fisheries Service, Western Region Office; Garrett County Chamber of Commerce; river flow and dam release information, (814) 533-8911.

3 Deep Creek Lake

Key species: Largemouth bass, smallmouth bass, yellow perch, walleye, chain pickerel, northern pike, and bluegill.

Deep Creek Lake is a well-known bass fishery.

Directions: From Baltimore, take the Beltway (Interstate 695) to Interstate 70 west and pick up Interstate 68 west near Hancock. From I-68, take U.S. Highway 219 south through McHenry. Pick up Rock Lodge Road south and then State Park Road to the park. Follow signs to the ramp.

DeLorme: *Maryland and Delaware Atlas & Gazetteer:* Page 65 C6.

Description: At 3,900 acres, Deep Creek Lake is Maryland's largest impoundment. The lake is 13 miles long, with 69 miles of shoreline. It has a maximum depth of about 75 feet near the dam and an average depth of about 25 feet. Deep Creek Lake contains a variety of fish habitat, from steep rocky shorelines near the dam to silt-bottomed shallow coves in the southern end, and supports a cold-water fishery for trout year-round. Submerged stumps and the many floating docks along the shoreline provide excellent cover for both largemouth and smallmouth bass as well as sunfish species.

Deep Creek Lake is located in a very touristy area. Every amenity imaginable is available.

The fishing: Deep Creek Lake is best known for its bass fishery. Both smallmouth and largemouth bass are common, though the "bucketmouths" get most of the attention. The quality of the bass fishery and the fact that gas-powered boats are permitted on this lake make it a popular site for bass-fishing tournaments.

Walleye are also common but take patience to catch. Yellow perch are abundant, too, and many anglers fish through the ice for them. Northern pike are available but not common; however, the chain pickerel are relatively easy to catch. Trophy-size bluegill are relatively common, with fish up to 11 inches caught.

At the time of this writing, the state records for bluegill, northern pike, and yellow perch were caught at Deep Creek Lake. Previous Maryland record fish from the lake have included walleye and brown trout.

Camping and lodging: Deep Creek Lake State Park has 112 campsites, 26 of which have electric hookups, that are available by reservation from spring through fall. Each site is conveniently located near heated restroom facilities complete with hot showers. A dump station for self-contained units is available. In addition, the park offers the Bear Den (an Adirondack-style shelter), two mini-camper cabins, and a yurt. The maximum length of stay for cabins and campsites is two weeks. Pets are permitted in certain designated loops.

For more information: Deep Creek Lake State Park; Maryland Department of Natural Resources, Fisheries Service, Western Region Office; Garrett County Chamber of Commerce.

4 Broadford Lake

Key species: Largemouth bass, smallmouth bass, crappie, bluegill and other sunfish, yellow perch, catfish, tiger muskie, and rainbow trout.

Directions: From Baltimore, take the Beltway (Interstate 695) to Interstate 70 west. Pick up Interstate 68 west near Hancock, then take U.S. Highway 219 south and turn left (east) on Kings Run Road. Proceed on Kings Run Road about 2 miles and turn right (south) on Deer Park Road, which becomes Broadford Road. Continue on Broadford Road to Maryland Highway 135, where you turn left (north) and proceed to the boat ramp sign on the left (west) side of the road.

DeLorme: Maryland and Delaware Atlas & Gazetteer: Page 64 A2.

Description: Public access is allowed along the entire shoreline of this 140-acre lake. Beaver work near deeper water provides excellent areas to fish for black crappie. The upper portion of the lake is shallow and contains submerged stumps, lily pads, and flats with heavy growths of aquatic vegetation, providing ideal habitat for largemouth bass and sunfish.

The fishing: This warm-water fishery supports a wide variety of species. Largemouth bass are the primary targets of most anglers, and quality-size fish are common. Smallmouth bass, bluegill, pumpkinseed, yellow perch, black crappie, yellow bullhead, and brown bullhead are also common. The smallmouths are usually caught around the riprap dam. The boat docks near the picnic area are a good place to fish for the bluegill and pumpkinseed.

Rainbow trout are stocked annually and add to the fishing opportunities. Tiger muskie are also stocked and are used to improve the predator/prey balance in the lake. These guys grow large in Broadford Lake and give anglers the chance at that once-in-a-lifetime fish.

Fly fishing with small poppers or bream busters for sunfish can be quite spectacular. Mosquito patterns are also effective. Use big bass bugs for largemouth and smallmouth bass. A bumble bee pattern works well.

Restrictions: Gasoline motors and ice fishing are prohibited on Broadford Lake. Access to the lake and facilities begins March 31 and runs through November 15. A user fee is charged at the entrance gate.

For more information: Maryland Department of Natural Resources, Fisheries Service, Western Region Office; Garrett County Chamber of Commerce.

5 North Branch of the Potomac River–Headwaters to Jennings Randolph Lake

Key species: Brown trout and rainbow trout.

Directions: This area of the North Branch delineates the border between Maryland and West Virginia. From Baltimore, take the Beltway (Interstate 695) to Interstate 70 west. Pick up Interstate 68 west near Hancock, then in Frostburg, take Maryland Highway 36 south through Westernport. Take Maryland Highway 46 west and pass into West Virginia. Follow MD 46 past the West Virginia shore of Jennings Randolph Lake to West Virginia Highway 42 west. This passes back into Maryland after crossing the North Branch near Kitzmiller.

DeLorme: Maryland and Delaware Atlas & Gazetteer: Page 64 B3.

Description: The North Branch of the Potomac runs southwest for about 25 miles to where it permanently leaves Maryland behind and becomes a West Virginia stream. Quite a few access locations are available to anglers all along its route.

This part of the river used to be highly polluted by acid from mine drainage. In fact, for fish populations, it was pretty much a dead zone. In 1993 the Maryland Department of Natural Resources (MDNR) began adding lime to the water, and though the acid has not been completely eliminated, the water quality has improved to the point where fish are again able to survive.

The fishing: If you want to fish for big trout in a wild setting, the upper North Branch is for you. Most of this part of the river is only accessible by floating or hiking; however, some areas can be reached easily from roadways. For those anglers willing to walk, the reward is the opportunity to fish in solitude. The MDNR Fisheries Service stocks remote areas from a tank truck that rides the railways, courtesy of the CSX Company through a cooperative agreement.

Early in the season, Woolly Buggers and brown midge patterns appear to work well for fly fishers. Minnow-like streamers are also effective. As the season warms, mosquito, gnat, and ant patterns become the favorites. Egg patterns, particularly sucker spawn flies, are the best for late-season fishing on the North Branch and its tributaries. Many anglers use large streamers if they are targeting 20-plus-inch trout. Leech patterns as well as Clousers, Zoo Cougars, and baitfish imitations all work at times.

Restrictions: The MDNR Fisheries Service initiated a trout-stocking program in two different management zones totaling 21 miles upstream of Jennings Randolph Lake. About 14 miles are stocked for harvest under put-and-take regulations, while about 7 miles within the Potomac State Forest are managed under delayed-harvest regulations. Always check the current regulations and appropriate signs to be sure of the rules for the area you intend to fish.

Camping: Much of this area of the Potomac runs through more than 11,000 acres of the Potomac State Forest. Many good campsites are available for a fee. Here are a few: Wallman/Laurel Run, south of Oakland, along Wallman and Laurel Run Roads leading to the North Branch (16 sites); Lostland Run, near the headquarters area, along Lostland Run Road leading to the North Branch (6 sites); primitive camping along forest roads, with one group site and one shelter site per area, along with roadside sites. Group sites (up to 20 persons) must be reserved in advance.

For more information: Potomac State Forest; Garrett County Chamber of Commerce.

6 North Branch of the Potomac River–Jennings Randolph Lake to Westernport

Key species: Brown trout, brook trout, and rainbow trout.

Directions: This area of the North Branch delineates the border between Maryland and West Virginia. From Baltimore, take the Beltway (Interstate 695) to Interstate 70 west. Pick up Interstate 68 west near Hancock, then in Frostburg, take Maryland Highway 36 south to Westernport. A number of trails and roads of various conditions give access to this part of the stream.

DeLorme: Maryland and Delaware Atlas & Gazetteer: Page 66 D2.

Description: This area is still quite wild. Jennings Randolph Lake (JRL), owned and operated by the Army Corps of Engineers, was completed and filled by 1982. The Corps manages the water quality downstream of the dam, and the Maryland Department of Natural Resources (MDNR) Fisheries Service stocks the river with several thousand trout annually.

The fishing: Many anglers fish the tailwater below the dam for trout. Depending on location and time, the stream is managed under put-and-take as well as catch-and-release regulations and is stocked with several thousand trout annually. The release from the dam remains very cold all summer, supporting year-round survival of trout for many miles downstream.

Because of the cold-water discharge, in addition to stocked trout, the North Branch downstream of JRL supports the natural reproduction of wild brook trout and brown trout, with some limited spawning by rainbow trout as well. Like the North Branch upstream of JRL, the tailwater area is beautiful and remote, with many opportunities for anglers to fish in solitude.

The North Branch downstream of JRL is a great place to raft-fish with a guide.

Camping: Much of this area of the Potomac runs through the Potomac State Forest. Many good campsites are available for a fee. Wallman/Laurel Run has 16 sites and is located south of Oakland along Wallman and Laurel Run Roads leading to the North Branch. Lostland Run has 6 sites and is located near the headquarters along Lostland Run Road leading to the North Branch. Group sites (up to 20 people) must be reserved in advance. Primitive camping is also available along forest roads.

For more information: Potomac State Forest; Garrett County Chamber of Commerce.

7 North Branch of the Potomac River–Westernport to Cumberland

Key species: Smallmouth bass.

Directions: From Baltimore, take the Beltway (Interstate 695) to Interstate 70 west. Pick up Interstate 68 near Hancock, then in Frostburg, take Maryland Highway 36 south to Westernport. A number of trails and roads of various conditions give access to this part of the stream.

DeLorme: Maryland and Delaware Atlas & Gazetteer: Page 67 C5.

Description: In the past, this portion of the river had water-quality problems, primarily due to effluent from a paper mill. With the cooperation of the mill company, the water quality has improved and now the fishing can be excellent in the 30-mile section between Westernport and Cumberland. This stretch of river is more populated, but this does not seem to affect the angling experience.

This is a really beautiful part of the Potomac, and the scenery is quite spectacular. The area is also quite remote, and many jagged cliffs tower above the West Virginia shore. Abundant wildlife can be observed around almost every bend.

Floating is the best way to enjoy fishing in this part of the river. Canoes, kayaks, and rafts are all suitable. Access is limited, and permission from landowners may be required.

The fishing: Smallmouth bass were absent because of the pollution but reintroduced in 1993 by the Maryland Department of Natural Resources (MDNR). By 1997 the fish had established a reproducing population, and the project was deemed a success. Presently, some of the best smallmouth fishing in Maryland is to be had in this part of the Potomac.

The trout fishery also improved because of the enhanced water quality in the North Branch. They are now showing up in much greater numbers.

Restrictions: Be sure to know the regulations when fishing this section of the North Branch. Because smallmouths are making a comeback, the regs are very strict. Check with the MDNR.

For more information: US Army Corps of Engineers, Baltimore District; Maryland Department of Natural Resources, Fisheries Service, Western Region Office.

8 Savage River Reservoir

Key species: Brook trout, brown trout, rainbow trout, largemouth bass, smallmouth bass, crappie, walleye, yellow perch, bluegill, and catfish.

Directions: From Baltimore, take the Beltway (Interstate 695) to Interstate 70 west.

Savage River Reservoir is a beautiful lake surrounded by mountains. Gas engines are not allowed.

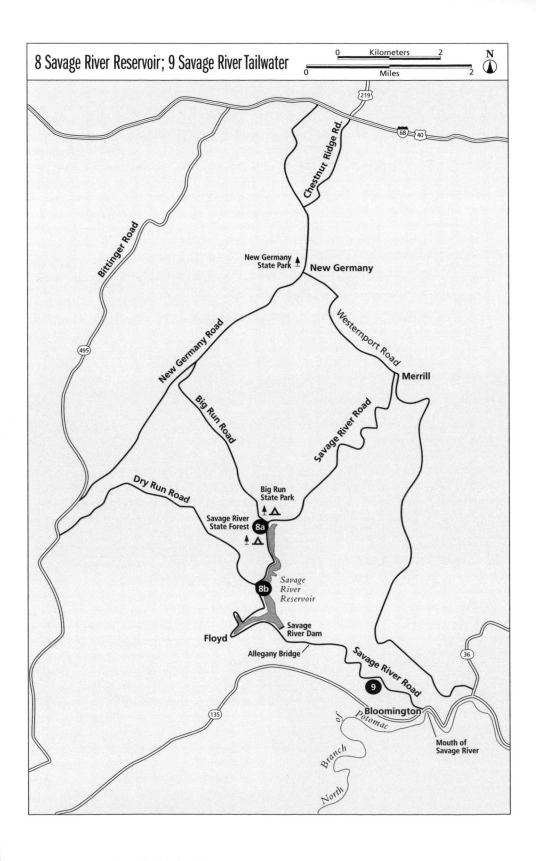

Kilometers

Miles

N

219

68 40

Chestnut Ridge Rd.

New Germany
State Park

New Germany

Bittinger Road

Westernport Road

Merrill

495

New Germany Road

Big Run Road

Savage River Road

Dry Run Road

Big Run
State Park

Savage River
State Forest

8a

*Savage
River
Reservoir*

8b

Floyd

Savage
River Dam

Allegany Bridge

Savage River Road

36

9

135

Bloomington

of Potomac

Branch

North

**Mouth of
Savage River**

Pick up Interstate 68 west near Hancock, then take exit 22, Chestnut Ridge Road, and head south. Turn left (south) on New Germany Road, then left (south) again on Big Run Road and follow it to the lake.

DeLorme: Maryland and Delaware Atlas & Gazetteer: Page 66 C2.

Accesses: **8a, Big Run State Park.** A boat ramp and access to the shoreline can be found at the end of Big Run Road.

8b, Dry Run Road. A ramp and access can be found at the end of Dry Run Road. To reach this access, continue south on New Germany Road past Big Run Road, which runs into Bittinger Road (Maryland Highway 495). Follow Bittinger to Dry Run Road and make a very sharp left, then follow Dry Run to the ramp at the end.

Description: This crystal clear lake is surrounded by mountains that rise steeply around it. The beautiful scenery makes this a great place to canoe or kayak. You are invited to launch your own canoe, kayak, or non-gasoline-powered craft to enjoy some of the best sport fishing in the county.

The fishing: The best fishing is done from a canoe or kayak. You may have to carry your craft to the lake, as the water is often low, but you will most likely encounter few others in the course of a day.

Restrictions: No gasoline motors.

Camping: Campsites are available at Big Run State Park and in the Savage River State Forest.

For more information: Big Run State Park; Savage River State Forest; Maryland Department of Natural Resources, Fisheries Service, Western Region Office; Garrett County Chamber of Commerce; water flow information, (410) 962-7687 or http://waterdata.usgs.gov/md/nwis/current/?type=flow.

9 Savage River Tailwater

Key species: Brook trout, brown trout, and rainbow trout.

Directions: From Baltimore, take the Beltway (Interstate 695) to Interstate 70 west. Pick up Interstate 68 west near Hancock, then take exit 22 and turn left (south) on Chestnut Ridge Road. Turn left (south) on New Germany Road, then left (south) again on Big Run Road. Travel to the end of Big Run Road and turn right (south) on Savage River Road. Continue around the Savage River Reservoir to the Savage River tailwater below the dam. Savage River Road parallels the river, and parking areas are marked.

Description: This is truly a beautiful area. Heavily wooded hillsides and wildflowers abound, adding to the fishing experience. The river has a moderate to steep gradient and averages about 55 feet in width. The bottom is composed mainly of boulders and cobble, providing excellent habitat for trout.

The fishing: Abundant native brook and brown trout and stocked brown trout are found in the Savage River tailwater. Rainbow trout can also be caught routinely in the tailwater; they either swim over the Savage River Reservoir Dam spillway or swim up from the North Branch of the Potomac River.

Many deep pools hold good trout, but be careful because algae can make the bottom slippery. Wear felt-soled or studded wading boots.

Flows vary, so be sure to call or check the Web before a fishing trip. Flows between 50 and 100 cubic feet per second (cfs) are considered good for fishing.

Restrictions: The regulation strategy includes a Fly Fishing Only Trophy Trout Management Area located in the section of the river from the Savage River Reservoir downstream 1.25 miles to the Allegany Bridge. Another Trophy Trout Management Area that is restricted to the use of artificial lures or flies is located between the Allegany Bridge and the mouth of the river, a distance of approximately 2.75 miles. Regulations for both Trophy Trout Management Areas include a year-round open season, a 12-inch minimum size limit for brook trout, an 18-inch minimum size limit for brown trout, and a two-trout daily creel limit. There is no minimum size limit on rainbow trout in either area.

Regulations change periodically, so please consult the *Maryland Freshwater Sportfishing Guide* for complete details.

For more information: Savage River State Forest; Maryland Department of Natural Resources, Fisheries Service, Western Region Office; Garrett County Chamber of Commerce; water flow information, (410) 962-7687 or http://waterdata.usgs.gov/md/nwis/current/?type=flow.

10 Casselman River

Key species: Brown trout and rainbow trout.

Directions: From Baltimore, take the Beltway (Interstate 695) to Interstate 70 west. Pick up Interstate 68 near Hancock, then take exit 19 north to Grantsville. Turn right (east) on alternate U.S. Highway 40 and proceed about 0.5 mile to Casselman River Bridge State Park on the left, or continue on alternate US 40 across a steel bridge and turn left on River Road. River Road parallels the Casselman to the Pennsylvania state line, about 5 miles. There are ample pull-offs along the road; please be respectful of the private-property owners that are allowing angler access.

DeLorme: Maryland and Delaware Atlas & Gazetteer: Page 66 A2.

Description: A fairly wide stream, the Casselman River offers long, productive riffle sections, deep runs, large deep holes, and pocket water. The substrate consists mainly of cobble-size stones, making wading here a bit easier than other Western Maryland rivers. This river runs through some very pretty scenery.

The fishing: The trout fishery in the Casselman River Delayed Harvest Trout Fishing Area is managed using adult hatchery brown and rainbow trout stocked each spring and fall. Many of these trout are truly trophy-size, with several bigger than 5 pounds! The Nemacolin Chapter of Trout Unlimited assists with float-stocking the stream, providing good fishing throughout the Delayed Harvest Trout Fishing Area.

Flows can fluctuate due to rainfall, especially during the spring, so please check for flow conditions. Flows less than 150 cubic feet per second (cfs) are considered good for fishing.

Restrictions: The Delayed Harvest Trout Fishing Area management scheme includes a catch-and-release season when anglers may use artificial lures or flies only. Anglers may harvest two trout per day during another part of the year when there are no bait or tackle restrictions. Regulations change, so please consult the *Maryland Freshwater Sportfishing Guide* for complete details and dates of each season.

For more information: Maryland Department of Natural Resources, Fisheries Service, Western Region Office; Garrett County Chamber of Commerce; water flow information, (410) 962-7687 or http://waterdata.usgs.gov/md/nwis/current/?type=flow.

11 Piney Reservoir

Key species: Largemouth bass, white crappie, tiger muskie, yellow perch, rock bass, pumpkinseed, brown bullhead, and rainbow trout.

Directions: From Baltimore, take the Beltway (Interstate 695) to Interstate 70 west. Pick up Interstate 68 west near Hancock and take the Finzel exit, Maryland Highway 546 north. Make an immediate left and proceed 0.25 mile to the stop sign at alternate U.S. Highway 40. Drive straight across alternate US 40 onto Piney Run Road and continue to the reservoir. Turn left (south) on the access road along the lake, and park in a designated area.

DeLorme: Maryland and Delaware Atlas & Gazetteer: Page 66 A3.

Description: Piney Reservoir is owned by the City of Frostburg and is its water supply. The surface area is 120 acres, with a maximum depth of 35 feet. The upper shallow end of the lake has a heavy growth of aquatic vegetation during the summer months, providing shelter for many of the lake's panfish. Near the lower portion, flooded standing timber provides some excellent largemouth bass habitat. Brush piles created by beavers along the shoreline offer very good areas to fish for white crappie. The rocky dam breast area is where the occasional walleye can be caught.

The fishing: Largemouth bass are the most popular game fish in this lake's diverse warm-water fishery. Many quality-size bucketmouths are present in the population. Bluegill, pumpkinseed, white crappie, rock bass, yellow perch, and brown bullhead are also quite plentiful and relatively easy to catch. In fact, angler harvest is encouraged.

Tiger muskie fingerlings are stocked to feed on the abundant panfish, which in turn improves panfish growth rates. This leads to a more desirable panfish population for the angler and provides a unique tiger muskie fishery. Some very large tigers have been caught, and many anglers are targeting these big fish exclusively.

Piney Reservoir is also a favorite spot for ice fishermen. Yellow perch are the most commonly caught fish through the ice, and they can provide some nonstop action! Rainbow trout are stocked each spring and fall to provide a two-season put-and-take trout fishery.

Restrictions: Boats are not allowed on Piney Reservoir, but there is public access along its entire shoreline. Check current regulations with the Maryland Department of Natural Resources.

For more information: Maryland Department of Natural Resources, Fisheries Service, Western Region Office; Garrett County Chamber of Commerce.

12 Town Creek

Key species: Brown trout, rainbow trout, smallmouth bass, and rock bass.

Directions: From Baltimore, take the Beltway (Interstate 695) to Interstate 70 west to Interstate 68 west. In Cumberland, take Maryland Highway 51 south for about 18.5 miles to Lower Town Creek Road and turn left. Continue 2.5 miles on Lower Town Creek Road, turn right on Maniford Road, and proceed to the state forest parking area on the right.

The Delayed Harvest Trout Fishing Area starts at a red post upstream of the parking area and continues downstream 1.75 miles to another red post. To access the upper area, continue on Lower Town Creek Road past Maniford Road about 1 mile to a low-water crossing. The lower boundary starts just upstream at the red post, and there is limited parking at this site. To access farther upstream, exercise extreme caution when fording the stream by vehicle. Continue 0.5 mile to a yellow pole gate on the left, park, and walk to the stream.

DeLorme: Maryland and Delaware Atlas & Gazetteer: Page 68 C2.

Description: Town Creek enters Maryland from Pennsylvania. It's a low-gradient stream, losing 360 feet of elevation in its 30-mile run to the Potomac River, an average drop of just 12 feet per mile. Large pools are common and are connected by productive riffle to white-water areas. The average width of the stream is about 50 feet, and the bottom is mostly cobble and scoured bedrock.

The fishing: Though this stream becomes too warm in the summer for trout survival, it is an excellent trout water in the spring, fall, and winter. Aquatic insect hatches are common, particularly in late winter, when stoneflies can provide fantastic early-season dry-fly fishing.

Many trophy-size brown and rainbow trout are stocked in the Town Creek Delayed Harvest Trout Fishing Areas in the spring and fall. The Nemacolin Chapter of Trout Unlimited assists with float-stocking the stream, providing good fishing throughout the delayed-harvest areas.

Smallmouth and rock bass and redbreast sunfish provide additional fishing opportunities, especially during the summer months.

Restrictions: The Delayed Harvest Trout Fishing Area management scheme includes a catch-and-release season from October 1 through June 15, when anglers may use artificial lures or flies only. Anglers may harvest two trout per day from June 16 through September 30, when there are no bait or tackle restrictions. Please consult the *Maryland Freshwater Sportfishing Guide* for complete details.

Camping: Green Ridge State Forest offers 100 designated primitive campsites located throughout 44,000 acres. Group sites are available, as well as sites located along the Potomac River and along the off-road vehicle trail. Pets are permitted on a leash. Camping permits may be obtained from the Green Ridge State Forest headquarters.

For more information: Green Ridge State Forest; Maryland Department of Natural Resources, Fisheries Service, Western Region Office.

13 Rocky Gap, also known as Lake Habeeb

Key species: Largemouth bass, walleye, crappie, channel and other catfish, bluegill and other sunfish, brown trout, and rainbow trout.

Directions: From Baltimore, take the Beltway (Interstate 695) to Interstate 70 west. Pick up Interstate 68 west near Hancock and continue to Rocky Gap State Park, exit 50.

DeLorme: Maryland and Delaware Atlas & Gazetteer: Page 68 A1.

Description: This lake has 9.4 miles of shoreline, and hiking trails provide anglers complete access. Various habitats are abundant: Shallow flats, points, and sharp drop-offs can all be productive. The lake's water is clear and has a maximum 74 feet. Artificial fish structures have been constructed and placed throughout the lake to increase survival of the young, as well as make it easier for anglers to locate their prey. During late summer, vegetation may hinder fishing and boating activities.

A boat ramp and boat rentals are available at the park, and children's fishing programs are offered throughout the summer season.

The fishing: This is an excellent largemouth bass lake, with fish up to 10 pounds. Smallmouth bass are available but in lesser numbers. Large bluegill, pumpkinseed, green sunfish, redbreast, and redear are readily caught. To add to the fine fishery, channel catfish have recently been stocked.

As part of the put-and-take trout program, browns and rainbows are stocked annually in Lake Habeeb. Other fish species you may encounter are golden, spotfin, and emerald shiners; bluntnose minnow; yellow bullhead; and black crappie.

Restrictions: Gas motors are prohibited. Check regularly with the Maryland Department of Natural Resources for size, season, and bag limit changes.

Camping and lodging: Rocky Gap State Park offers 278 individual campsites (including 30 with electric hookups), a family group site, three youth group camping areas, a dump station, bathhouses, a laundry, and a camp store. Pets are allowed in two designated camp loops. Ten mini-cabins, each with electricity, bunk bed, and double bed, are also available for rent, in addition to a three-bedroom chalet with a completely furnished kitchen, wraparound deck, fireplace, outdoor campfire area, and grill.

For more information: Rocky Gap State Park; Maryland Department of Natural Resources, Fisheries Service, Lewistown Work Center.

14 Blair Valley Lake

Key species: Largemouth bass, tiger muskie, bluegill, crappie, redear sunfish, yellow perch, carp, and brown bullhead.

Directions: From Baltimore, take the Beltway (Interstate 695) to Interstate 70 west. Past Hagerstown, take Maryland Highway 68 north (exit 18) to Clear Spring. Proceed straight through the intersection on MD 68 and turn right on Broadfording Road, then make a left on Blair Valley Road and follow it to the Indian Springs Wildlife Management Area. Turn left into the parking lot and ramp area.

DeLorme: Maryland and Delaware Atlas & Gazetteer: Page 70 A3.

Description: Depending on conditions, Blair Valley Lake covers between 22 and 32 acres. The average depth is 10 feet, while the deepest part near the dam is 18 feet.

Phytoplankton blooms are common, and oxygen becomes depleted below 8 feet during the summer months. Submerged aquatic vegetation provides the primary cover for fish. Artificial cover is also added.

A free boat ramp and parking lot are available.

The fishing: This lake is managed as a warm-water fishery. Some nice bass are caught each year, and tiger muskie over 40 inches are available. Black crappie, redear sunfish, yellow perch, brown bullhead, and carp are relatively easy to catch. Adult rainbow trout are stocked during the spring and fall to provide a popular put-and-take fishery.

Restrictions: Electric trolling motors are permitted, but gas motors are prohibited. Trophy Bass Regulations (slot limit) are in effect; consult the *Maryland Freshwater Sportfishing Guide.* Tiger muskie are subject to a 36-inch minimum size and a one-per-day creel limit.

For more information: Maryland Department of Natural Resources, Fisheries Service, Lewistown Work Center.

15 Greenbrier State Park

Key species: Brown trout, largemouth bass, and bluegill.

Directions: From Baltimore, take the Beltway (Interstate 695) to Interstate 70 west to exit 42. Bear right on Maryland Highway 17 north (follow signs) and proceed to the center of Myersville, where MD 17 turns right. Follow MD 17 to the flashing lights at the intersection of U.S. Highway 40 and turn left (west). Follow US 40 through Jerusalem to the park, which is on the left (south) side of the road.

DeLorme: Maryland and Delaware Atlas & Gazetteer: Page 71 C6.

Description: Hiking trails—including the Appalachian Trail, which passes through the park—and wildlife viewing are popular activities at Greenbrier. It is a multi-use park, providing many kinds of recreation.

Located in the Appalachian Mountains, the park's hiking trails meander through a variety of wildlife habitats and afford a view of the area's geological history. There are picnic tables, grills, and playgrounds in the day-use area, and a boat ramp and boat rentals are available. All in all, this is a nice family retreat for a long weekend.

The fishing: The 42-acre freshwater lake is stocked with hatchery trout, largemouth bass, and bluegill. This is a great place to fish from a canoe or the bank.

Restrictions: Fishing with live minnow is not permitted.

Camping: The park has 165 campsites, 40 with electric hookups, offering conveniently located bathhouses with hot showers. Each campsite is equipped with a parking area, table, and fire ring (fires must be kept inside the rings). A dump station is available. Senior citizens with a valid Golden Age Pass receive a half-price discount on camping when staying Sunday through Thursday.

For more information: Greenbrier State Park; Maryland Department of Natural Resources, Fisheries Service, Western Region Office.

16 Big Hunting Creek

Key species: Brown trout and brook trout.

Directions: From Baltimore, take the Beltway (Interstate 695) to Interstate 70 west. In Frederick, take U.S. Highway 15 north to Thurmont. Exit onto Maryland Highway 77 west to the state and national parks. MD 77 follows Big Hunting Creek; look for designated parking areas.

From Hagerstown, take Interstate 70 east to exit 35. Follow Maryland Highway 66 north to Smithsburg and turn right on Maryland Highway 64 north. Then turn right on Maryland Highway 77 east, follow it over Catoctin Mountain to the state and national parks, and look for designated parking areas.

DeLorme: Maryland and Delaware Atlas & Gazetteer: Page 72 B2.

Description: Big Hunting Creek is a small freestone stream. It's just 10 feet wide at the headwaters above Cunningham Falls and 20 feet wide at the lower park boundary. The stream is shaded throughout, and the habitat varies. Shallow riffles, small plunge pools, long runs, and ample pocket water with many large boulders continually challenge fly casters. The upper third of the tailwater has a gentle gradient with slow runs and a meandering channel. Farther downstream the gradient increases, and there is an abundance of plunge pools and pocket water.

The fishing: Most anglers come to Big Hunting Creek to fly fish for wild brown trout, since it is one of the best waters in the state for this species. Browns are found throughout the watershed, from the tiny headwaters downstream through the town of Thurmont. They can grow to about 15 inches in this stream, but the majority are less than 12 inches.

Wild brook trout are limited to the Hauver Branch and Big Hunting Creek upstream of Cunningham Falls Reservoir; no trout are stocked in these areas.

Two organizations, the Potomac Valley Fly Fishermen and the Maryland Fly Anglers, raise or purchase rainbow and brook trout, respectively, and stock the Big Hunting Creek tailwater each spring as part of the Co-operative Trout Rearing Program. Many of these hatchery fish weigh more than a pound, offering anglers variety and a chance to catch a large trout.

Restrictions: Big Hunting Creek and its tributaries within Cunningham Falls State Park and Catoctin Mountain Park are restricted to catch-and-release, fly-fishing-only restrictions. Please consult the *Maryland Freshwater Sportfishing Guide* for details.

Camping and lodging: Cunningham Falls State Park has two camping areas with a total of about 170 sites, some with electric hookups. Bathhouses with hot showers are available, and each campsite has a parking area, table, fire ring, and lantern post. A camp store offers groceries, camping supplies, and souvenirs. Winter camping is available in the Manor Area from November 1 until the end of firearm deer-hunting season. The shower building is closed starting November 1, but a portable toilet and water source are available.

Catoctin Mountain Park also has two camping areas. Owens Creek Campground is open April 15 through the third Sunday in November; sites are available on a first come, first served basis. Pets are permitted on leash. Poplar Grove Youth Group Tent Campground is open year-round, except March 1 through April 15, for adult-supervised organized youth groups whose members are under age 18; reservations are required. There are three sites within Poplar Grove, each accommodating up to 25 people.

The National Park Service also offers the following three cabin areas, by reservation only: Camp Misty Mount, a cabin rental facility for individuals, families, or small groups, is open mid-April through the end of October. Camp Greentop may be rented by organized groups of 60 people or more during the week or on weekends from April through mid-June and mid-August through the end of October.

Camp Round Meadow is a group camp with four dorms that can sleep 30 people each and is open all year. A dining hall seating 120 people is included. Additional facilities include a gym with a basketball court, a small outdoor gazebo, and a conference room.

For more information: Cunningham Falls State Park; Catoctin Mountain (National) Park; Maryland Department of Natural Resources, Fisheries Service, Lewistown Work Center.

17 Cunningham Falls Reservoir, also known as Hunting Creek Lake

Key species: Largemouth bass, bluegill and other sunfish, crappie, stocked trout, and catfish.

Directions: From Baltimore, take the Beltway (Interstate 695) to Interstate 70 west. In Frederick, take U.S. Highway 15 north to Thurmont, then take Maryland Highway 77 west to Cunningham Falls State Park and turn left (south) on Catoctin Hollow Road. You will see the lake on your right; turn right into the parking lot.

DeLorme: Maryland and Delaware Atlas & Gazetteer: Page 72 B2.

Description: Cunningham Falls Reservoir covers 42 acres and has a maximum depth of approximately 75 feet. Shallow water and a muddy bottom characterize the upper third of the lake. Steep rocky shorelines and deeper water are found in the lower end of the lake. Rocky banks, fallen trees, beaver lodges, and submerged aquatic vegetation provide abundant cover. In addition, some artificial habitat (terra-cotta drain tile, evergreen trees, pallet structures) has also been constructed in recent years.

A paved boat ramp with dock (a fee applies) as well as a wheelchair-accessible fishing pier is available. Due to the potential for low water levels during the late summer and fall, anglers with trailered boats should call the park before their trip to make sure the ramp is usable.

The fishing: Cunningham Falls Reservoir is a warm-water fishery. Largemouth bass up to 6 pounds are fairly common, and panfish (bluegill, redear, black crappie) upwards of 10 inches are also caught regularly. Adult trout are stocked during the spring and fall to provide a popular put-and-take resource.

Restrictions: Gas motors are prohibited, but electric motors are permitted.

Camping: Cunningham Falls State Park has two camping areas with a total of about 170 sites, some with electric hookups. Bathhouses with hot showers are available, and each campsite has a parking area, table, fire ring, and lantern post. A camp store offers groceries, camping supplies, and souvenirs. Winter camping is available in the Manor Area from November 1 until the end of firearm deer-hunting season. The shower building is closed starting November 1, but a portable toilet and water source are available.

For more information: Cunningham Falls State Park; Maryland Department of Natural Resources, Fisheries Service, Lewistown Work Center.

18 Owens Creek

Key species: Brown trout, brook trout, and rainbow trout.

Directions: From Baltimore, take the Beltway (Interstate 695) to Interstate 70 west. In Frederick, take U.S. Highway 15 north to Thurmont, then take Maryland Highway 550 west. MD 550 parallels Owens Creek; look for parking areas posted with regulation signs.

DeLorme: Maryland and Delaware Atlas & Gazetteer: Page 72 B2.

Description: Owens Creek is a fairly high-gradient stream with a boulder and cobble substrate throughout. Occasional large pools separate extensive fast runs and pocket water. Undercut banks and woody debris provide additional habitat. Summer and fall flows can be very low.

The fishing: Anglers can fish for wild or hatchery trout in Owens Creek. Native brook trout dominate the headwaters, while a small population of wild browns can be found throughout. Hatchery rainbow and brown trout are stocked each spring from the bridge on Foxville/Deerfield Road downstream to the covered bridge on Roddy Road, with the exception of a posted section above and below the intersection of Eylers Valley Flint Road and MD 550. The degree of over-summer survival will vary with conditions; exceedingly hot and/or dry summers will result in reduced habitat and survival.

Fly fishing during April, May, and June can be particularly productive. These trout are not usually very selective, but they will spook from a noisy approach.

Restrictions: From the headwaters downstream to Raven Rock Road, a two-trout-per-day creel limit is in effect with no tackle restrictions. This area is managed for wild trout, and no trout are stocked. From Raven Rock Road downstream to Roddy Road, put-and-take/catch-and-release regulations are in effect. Under these regulations, anglers fishing from June 1 through the end of February must use artificial lures and release all trout caught. During March, April, and May, put-and-take regulations, closures, and creel limits apply. Please consult the *Maryland Freshwater Sportfishing Guide* for details.

For more information: Maryland Department of Natural Resources, Fisheries Service, Lewistown Work Center.

Northeastern Maryland and Washington, D.C.

Though quite urban and populated, the metropolitan area around Washington, D.C., and Baltimore holds some surprisingly excellent and diverse angling. Whether you are interested in fine saltwater fishing for striped bass (rockfish) and other game species, or river angling for largemouth or smallmouth bass, or just a lazy day on a pond or lake casting for bream, bass, or crappie, this region has it all. One can even find some excellent fly fishing for trout here.

This chapter includes the District of Columbia, the city of Baltimore, and the following Maryland counties: all of Baltimore, Harford, Montgomery, Carroll, and Howard, and parts of Cecil, Anne Arundel, Prince William, and Frederick.

The boundaries of this chapter are everything east of a line drawn north–south through Frederick, and north of a line drawn east–west from the southern tip of DC to Annapolis.

19 Potomac River–Edwards Ferry

Key species: Largemouth bass, smallmouth bass, crappie, catfish, American eel, tiger muskie, redbreast sunfish, and carp.

Directions: From Washington, take the Capitol Beltway (Interstate 495) to Maryland Highway 190 west (River Road), which eventually becomes Mount Nebo Road. Follow this road to Edwards Ferry Road, turn left (south), and proceed to the boat ramp at the end.

DeLorme: Maryland and Delaware Atlas & Gazetteer: Page 54 D1.

The fishing: Excellent angling is available in this part of the Upper Potomac. Try crankbaits and plastics for smallmouths and swimming plugs for bucketmouths. Large redbreast sunfish can be caught on worms and grubs. Carp anglers fish from the bank with corn or prepared baits.

For more information: Maryland Department of Natural Resources, Wildlife & Heritage Service, Bel Air Regional Office.

20 Clopper Lake–Seneca Creek State Park

Key species: Largemouth bass, crappie, bluegill and other sunfish, and channel catfish.

Directions: From Washington, take the Capitol Beltway (Interstate 495) to Interstate 270 north and exit onto Maryland Highway 124 west (Quince Orchard Road). Turn right on Maryland Highway 117 (Clopper Road). The entrance to Seneca Creek State Park is on the left off Clopper Road.

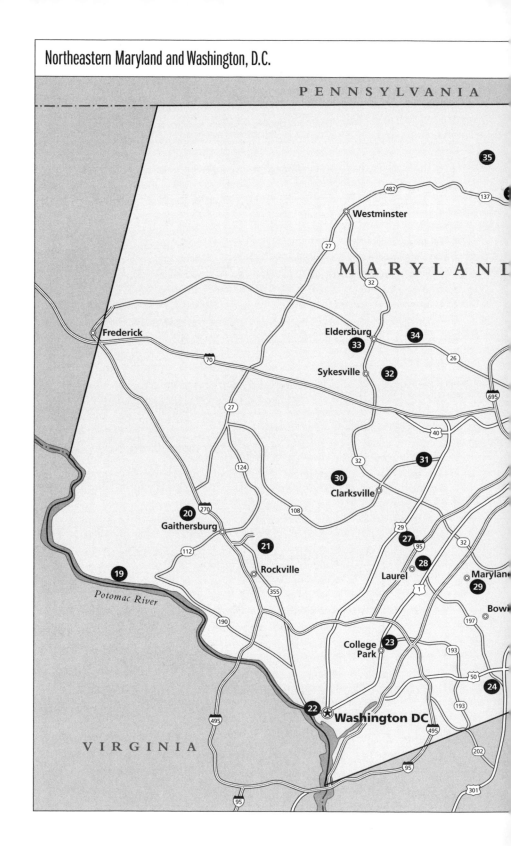

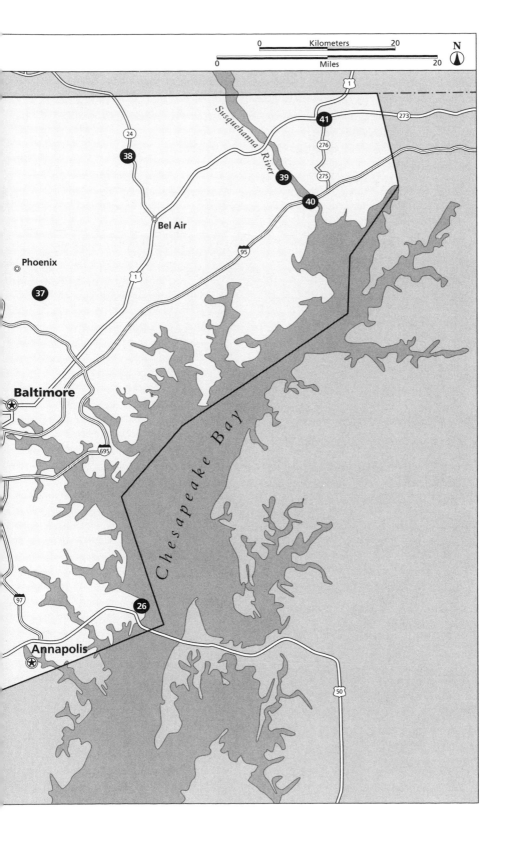

DeLorme: Maryland and Delaware Atlas & Gazetteer: Page 54 D2.

Description: Clopper Lake has abundant submerged aquatic vegetation that can become quite dense during the summer and early fall. It averages 18 feet in depth, with a number of shallow coves. Fallen trees and beaver lodges provide habitat for crappie, sunfish, and largemouth bass.

Private boats are allowed, except on weekends and holidays in the summer, and boat rentals are available.

The fishing: Clopper Lake's bass are overabundant, but specimens upwards of 12 inches are available to anglers. Channel catfish do well in Clopper, and some large "catties" are regularly caught. Quality-size redear sunfish, as well as bluegill and pumpkinseed, are also available and relatively easy to catch. Black crappie, some up to 10 inches, may also be taken.

Tiger muskie fingerlings, a hybrid cross of northern pike and muskellunge, have been stocked into Clopper Lake. Anglers have reported catching tigers, suggesting some success with their survival, but very few have been caught as of this writing. Other species found in Clopper are brown bullhead and common carp.

Camping: There is no camping at Seneca Creek State Park.

For more information: Seneca Creek State Park.

21 Lake Needwood

Key species: Largemouth bass, bluegill, and rainbow trout.

Directions: From Washington, take the Capitol Beltway (Interstate 495) to Maryland Highway 355 north. Turn right (northeast) on Redland Road, then right (east) again on Needwood Road and follow it to the park.

DeLorme: Maryland and Delaware Atlas & Gazetteer: Page 46 A3.

Description: Lake Needwood covers 75 acres and is part of Rock Creek Regional Park. Rowboats, canoes, and pedal boats are available for rent. You can also take a ride on the *Needwood Queen*, a flat-bottom pontoon boat.

The fishing: Nice bass and bluegill are caught here. Rainbow trout are stocked and offer some good fishing for urban anglers.

For more information: Rock Creek Regional Park; Montgomery County Department of Parks.

22 Potomac River–Metropolitan Washington, D.C.

Key species: Largemouth bass, crappie, bluegill and other sunfish, carp, American eel, catfish, yellow perch, white perch, chain pickerel, shad, northern pike, walleye, and striped bass.

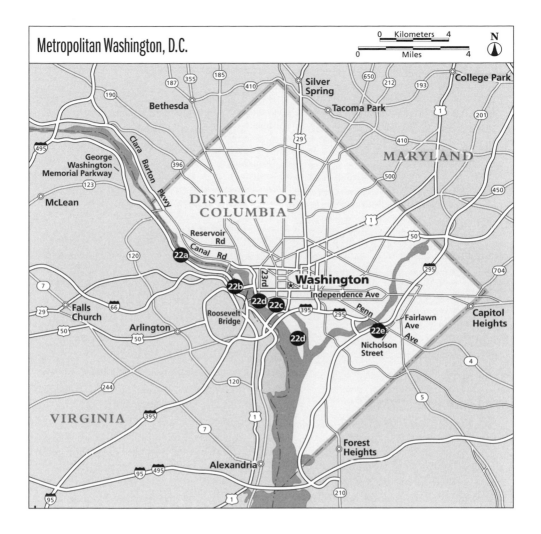

Metropolitan Washington, D.C.

Kilometers 4

Miles 4

N

College Park

Silver Spring

Bethesda

Tacoma Park

George Washington Memorial Parkway

McLean

MARYLAND

DISTRICT OF COLUMBIA

Reservoir Rd

Canal Rd

22a

23rd

Washington

Independence Ave

22b

22d 22c

Falls Church

Roosevelt Bridge

Arlington

Penn

Fairlawn Ave

Capitol Heights

22d

22e

Nicholson Street

VIRGINIA

Forest Heights

Alexandria

Directions: Canal Road, MacArthur Boulevard, and Clara Barton Parkway all run along the Potomac in DC.

DeLorme: *Maryland and Delaware Atlas & Gazetteer:* Pages 46 C2 and 47 D4.

Accesses: **22a, Fletcher's Boat House.** From Interstate 495, take the Glen Echo exit east; you will be on the Clara Barton Parkway. Follow the parkway until it becomes Canal Road and continue on Canal until Reservoir Road. The canal is just ahead of you. The entrance is on the right (west) side of the road. A boat ramp and shore fishing are available here.

22b, Theodore Roosevelt Island. You can only get here from the northbound lanes of the George Washington Memorial Parkway. The entrance is just north of the Roosevelt Bridge. You can also go by Metro; the closest station is Rosslyn.

22c, Tidal Basin. Located on the south side of Independence Avenue.

22d, East and West Potomac Parks. Located at the south end of 23rd Street (the parks are within walking distance of each other).

22e, Anacostia Park. From the northern end of Interstate 295 south, keep to the center lane and take the eastbound Pennsylvania Avenue exit, then take the first right onto Fairlawn Avenue. Go to the stop sign and turn right on Nicholson Street to enter the park.

Description: The Potomac, even as it runs through DC, is considered one of the most beautiful rivers on the East Coast. Many parks are available to the angler in the metropolitan area.

DC's Fisheries and Wildlife Division runs the Summer Fishing Program, a two-day educational and recreational program for kids and adults. Aquatic biology, ecology, conservation, and ethical angling are stressed. Call (202) 535-2260 for details.

The fishing: Fishing in DC may seem strange to many, but since the Potomac has been cleaned up, angling has improved to the point where it is good, if not excellent.

For more information: DC Department of Health, Fisheries and Wildlife Division; Fletcher's Boat House; Anacostia Park.

23 Lake Artemesia

Key species: Largemouth bass and bluegill.

Directions: From Washington, take the Capitol Beltway (Interstate 495) to exit 23, Kenilworth Avenue south (Maryland Highway 201), and turn right (west) on Greenbelt Road (Maryland Highway 193). Turn right (north) on Branchville Road, which becomes Ballew Avenue, and follow it to the stop sign at Berwyn Road; across the road is the parking lot.

DeLorme: Maryland and Delaware Atlas & Gazetteer: Page 47 B5.

Description: This 38-acre lake is in the metro DC area. Besides fishing, the Lake Artemesia Natural Area boasts a few miles of hiking trails.

The fishing: This urban lake has surprisingly excellent fishing for bluegill and bucketmouths. A few crappie are also available for those who target this species.

For more information: Lake Artemesia Natural Area; Maryland Department of Natural Resources, Fisheries Service, Central Region Office.

24 Allen Pond

Key species: Largemouth bass, channel catfish, crappie, and bluegill.

Directions: From Baltimore, take the Beltway (Interstate 695) to Interstate 97 south.

Exit at Maryland Highway 3 south, which becomes U.S. Highway 301 near Bowie. From US 301, make a right (west) on Maryland Highway 197, then a left (south) on Mitchellville Road. Turn right (west) on Northview Drive; the park is on the left (south) side of the road.

From Washington take U.S. Highway 50 east and exit south onto US 301. Go south on US 301, make a right (west) on MD 197, then a left (south) on Mitchellville Road. Turn right (west) on Northview Drive; the park is on the left (south) side of the road.

DeLorme: Maryland and Delaware Atlas & Gazetteer: Page 48 C1.

Description: Allen Pond is a great place to take the family for a day. Besides fishing, visitors will find a playground, walking trail, ball fields, volleyball courts, and picnic areas. The Allen Pond park is run by the City of Bowie. Boats are available for rent; permits are necessary to use your own boat.

The fishing: Some fine bass are taken at Allen Pond, and crappie fishing is also good. Fishing from a boat is possible, and a paved walkway gives access to much of the shoreline.

Allen Pond is a favorite destination for spring crappie.

For more information: Maryland Department of Natural Resources, Wildlife & Heritage Service, Prince Frederick Office; Bowie City Hall.

25 Governor's Bridge Natural Area and Canoe Launch

Key species: Largemouth bass and bluegill.

Directions: From Baltimore, take the Beltway (Interstate 695) to Interstate 97 south. Exit at Maryland Highway 3 south, which becomes U.S. Highway 301 near Bowie. From US 301, make a left (east) on Governor's Bridge Road; the park entrance is on the right.

From Washington take U.S. Highway 50 to US 301. Go south on US 301 and make a left (east) on Governor's Bridge Road. For the launch ramp, go past the park entrance to the gravel road on the right and follow it to the landing.

DeLorme: Maryland and Delaware Atlas & Gazetteer: Page 48 C1.

Description: This area not only gives access to the Patuxent River, but also has an 8-acre lake that is quite productive. Located near the Bowie Baysox Stadium, Governor's Bridge Natural Area was once an active sand- and gravel-mining operation. In the 1980s the property was selected as a "mitigation" site, and a restoration plan was developed to return the land to its natural environment. The park is managed as catch-and-release for bass.

Once the initial launch point for the Patuxent River Water Trail, Governor's Bridge provides access to the river for canoes and kayaks. The area is susceptible to seasonal flooding, so call ahead. Parking is available.

The fishing: The lake supports many good-size largemouth bass. Access is easy from the loop trail that encircles the lake.

Restrictions: A special-use permit or advance reservation is required for all activities. Access is restricted. Check current regulations with the Maryland Department of Natural Resources.

For more information: Governor's Bridge Natural Area and Canoe Launch.

26 Sandy Point State Park

Key species: Striped bass, white perch, bluefish, spot, and croaker.

Directions: From Baltimore, take the Beltway (Interstate 695) to Interstate 97 south. In Annapolis, pick up U.S. Highway 50 east. Exit immediately before the Bay Bridge at Holly Beach Farm Road and follow the signs to the park.

DeLorme: Maryland and Delaware Atlas & Gazetteer: Page 49 B4.

Description: This 786-acre park is located on the western shore of Chesapeake Bay just north of the Bay Bridge. It has beautiful beaches with great views and, in addition to fishing, offers boating, swimming, bird- and wildlife-watching, and picnic areas.

The park provides a fine multi-boat launch ramp. This is a great place to launch for fishing around the Bay Bridge and other middle-bay hotspots.

The fishing: Striped bass and white perch are the primary targets of those fishing out of Sandy Point. Anglers can pursue their sport from a jetty, beach, pier, or boat.

Camping: There is no camping at Sandy Point State Park.

For more information: Sandy Point State Park.

27 Rocky Gorge Reservoir, also known as T. H. Duckett Reservoir

Key species: Largemouth bass, smallmouth bass, striped bass, tiger muskie, walleye, crappie, channel catfish, yellow perch, white perch, bluegill, and carp.

Directions: From Baltimore, take the Beltway (Interstate 695) to Interstate 95 south. Take exit 33 west to Sandy Spring Road, then turn right (north) on Riding Stable Road, which becomes Brooklyn Bridge Road. The access to the reservoir is on the left (north).

From Washington, take the Capitol Beltway (Interstate 495) to Interstate 95 north. Take exit 33 west to Sandy Spring Road, then turn right (north) on Riding Stable Road, which becomes Brooklyn Bridge Road. The access to the reservoir is on the left (north).

DeLorme: Maryland and Delaware Atlas & Gazetteer: Page 47 A5.

Description: Rocky Gorge is operated by the Washington Suburban Sanitary Commission and is the water source for suburban DC municipalities. It was formed by the Duckett Dam across the Patuxent River. Some areas reach depths of over 100 feet, but the average is 33 feet. The lake covers more than 800 acres and has about 12 miles of shoreline.

The fishing: Fishing is good throughout Rocky Gorge; however, the areas in the northern sections seem to warm faster. The coves are also early-season hotspots, especially when the bluegill start spawning. Bass will patrol the area looking for an easy meal.

Minnows and crankbaits are favorites with Rocky Gorge anglers. Fly fishers like small poppers and bream busters.

Restrictions: Fishing is allowed from sunrise to one hour past sunset. Boating is allowed March 1 through December 31; no gasoline engines. Swimming is not permitted.

Shore fishing is allowed only from the following areas:

- Along the west bank only, parallel to Tucker Lane, south from Maryland Highway 108 approximately 650 yards to the "No Trespassing" signs.
- Scott's Cove adjacent to all parking lots, along the perimeter east and west to the "No Trespassing" signs.
- Along the left or north bank of the reservoir from Brown's Bridge Road down-

stream, a distance of approximately 450 yards to the sign. Along the south bank from Brown's Bridge Road upstream about 300 yards to the sign. Also, upstream and downstream of these respective points to the "No Trespassing" signs.

• Along the right or south bank from the end of Supplee Lane west to the sign. East to the "No Trespassing" signs.

A Watershed Use Permit is required, which may be obtained at the following locations: Brighton Dam Visitors' Information Center, located at the top of the dam, adjacent to the parking lot; open for permit sales daily from 8:00 a.m. to 8:00 p.m., including holidays.

Richard G. Hocevar Building, Cashier's Office, Lobby Level, Room 1072, 14501 Sweitzer Lane, Laurel; permits may be obtained weekdays from 7:30 a.m. to 5:00 p.m. (closed holidays).

For additional permit information, call Brighton Dam, (301) 774-9124.

For more information: Washington Suburban Sanitary Commission.

28 Laurel Lake

Key species: Largemouth bass, channel catfish, bluegill, and redear sunfish.

Directions: From Washington, take U.S. Highway 1 north to Laurel and turn left (west) on Cherry Lane.

DeLorme: Maryland and Delaware Atlas & Gazetteer: Page 47 A5.

Description: This suburban, 11-acre pond is set right in the middle of a bunch of shopping malls. Most of the shoreline is accessible to anglers. Boat rentals are available.

The fishing: Though surrounded by development, this pond yields some nice bass and channel cats up to 6 pounds. It's a nice place to take the kids for a day of bluegill fishing.

For more information: Laurel Parks & Recreation Department.

29 Patuxent National Wildlife Refuge

Key species: Bluegill, smallmouth bass, largemouth bass, catfish, black crappie, pickerel, stocked trout, shad, chub, carp, sucker, striped bass, and yellow perch.

Directions: From Washington, take the Capitol Beltway (Interstate 495) to the Baltimore-Washington Parkway north. Turn right (east) on Powder Mill Road, then right (east) again on Scarlet Tangier Loop and follow it to the visitor center.

DeLorme: Maryland and Delaware Atlas & Gazetteer: Page 47 B6.

Description: The research refuge is spread over a large area near Laurel and Maryland City.

The fishing: Refuge visitors may fish within the North Tract at Lake Allen, New Marsh, Cattail Pond, Rieve's Pond, Bailey Bridge Marsh, and the Little Patuxent River. In addition, visitors may fish at Cash Lake, which has a nice pier available.

Restrictions: Fishing seasons and hours vary by location. The North Tract is open all year to fishing during operating hours; some exceptions apply. Cash Lake is open to fishing June 11 through October 14 from 6:00 a.m. to 8:00 p.m. during June, July, and August, and from 7:00 a.m. to 6:30 p.m. during September and October. This may change, so check current regulations.

For more information: U.S. Fish and Wildlife Service, National Wildlife Visitor Center.

30 Triadelphia Reservoir

Key species: Largemouth bass, smallmouth bass, striped bass, tiger muskie, walleye, crappie, channel catfish, yellow perch, white perch, bluegill, and carp.

Directions: From Baltimore, take the Beltway (Interstate 695) to Interstate 70 west. Take exit 87, U.S. Highway 29 (Columbia Pike) south, then turn right (west) on Maryland Highway 108 (Clarksville Pike). In Clarksville, turn right on Brighton Dam Road. Turn right (north) on New Hampshire Avenue, then right (east) on Green Ridge Road and follow it to the boat ramp.

DeLorme: Maryland and Delaware Atlas & Gazetteer: Page 57 C4.

Description: This medium-size lake covers 800 acres and is 65 feet at its deepest point. The entire lake is tree-lined and usually not very crowded. It's a pleasant place near metro DC.

The fishing: Largemouth bass are the primary quarry of those who fish Triadelphia.
  Shad-colored spinnerbaits and ½-ounce jigs work well when the fish are deep. Plenty of wood cover is available for hiding. Many anglers use Texas-rigged worms when fishing shallow water.
  Fly fishing is quite popular here, and even carp are occasionally caught on flies. Big bass bugs and poppers work well. Deer-hair frogs in yellow and green can catch fish at times, especially when the cicadas are hatching.

Restrictions: Fishing is legal from sunrise to an hour past sunset, and a permit is required. Shore fishing is allowed only from the following areas:

• Where Greenbridge Road terminates at the reservoir in Montgomery County, east and west along the shoreline to the "No Trespassing" signs.
• On the south bank of Pigtail Branch along Greenbridge-Dayton Road in Howard County to the "No Trespassing" signs.
• Where Triadelphia Lake Road terminates at the reservoir in Montgomery County, west to Georgia Avenue (Maryland Highway 97) and east to the sign indicating the designated fishing boundary.

• On the south bank of Big Branch below the bridge on Triadelphia Mill Road in Howard County to the "No Trespassing" signs.

For more information: Washington Suburban Sanitary Commission; Brighton Dam Visitor Center, (301) 774-9124.

31 Centennial Lake

Key species: Largemouth bass, tiger muskie, channel catfish, crappie, bluegill, and stocked rainbow trout.

Directions: From Baltimore, take the Beltway (Interstate 695) to Interstate 70 west. Take exit 87, U.S. Highway 29 (Columbia Pike) south, then take Maryland Highway 108 west. The main entrance to Centennial Park is 1 mile on the right.

DeLorme: Maryland and Delaware Atlas & Gazetteer: Page 57 C5.

Description: Centennial Lake is a small suburban impoundment that is usually clear but can become murky following storms. Algae blooms are common as a result of increased nutrient loads from storm-related runoff and during the fall as aquatic vegetation dies off. The lake contains submerged aquatic vegetation during the warm months of the year, which can become a nuisance to shoreline anglers, and beds of lily pads are expanding in many locations around its perimeter.

Centennial Lake is relatively shallow, with a mean depth of 10.2 feet, and contains several small, shallow coves. Downed trees from the surrounding forested buffer provide additional habitat. The lake is encircled by a paved path that provides anglers with access to nearly the entire perimeter.

A seasonal boat ramp is available for launching craft. Rowboats and canoes can be rented from the boathouse.

The fishing: This lake has too many largemouth bass, so they grow slowly. However, many over 12 inches are available to anglers, and population surveys have revealed some up to 6½ pounds. Rainbow trout have been stocked in Centennial Lake since 1992 as part of the state's put-and-take trout program. These fish are a popular target and run between 9 and 20 inches.

Tiger muskie fingerlings have also been stocked in the lake, and fish over 36 inches are now swimming in it. Channel catfish have been stocked, too, and many large ones are taken each year. Fishing for channel cats is most successful during the early morning hours and the late evening before the park closes.

Centennial Lake provides quality-size bluegill, pumpkinseed, and redear sunfish. They can be found throughout the lily pads, especially during the fall. Black crappie round out the list of fish species available to anglers, with nice-size ones (9 to 12 inches) available.

Restrictions: Centennial Park is open from 7:00 a.m. to dusk, or as posted. The boat ramp is open March through November. All boats are required to have a boating permit; daily and seasonal permits may be purchased at the boathouse.

Only Class A boats are allowed, 16 feet or less in length, with electric motors. The west end of the lake is marked by buoys and is designated a wildlife sanctuary, which means fishing is off-limits. Be sure to check current regulations for all species before fishing.

For more information: Howard County Recreation and Parks.

32 Patapsco River

Key species: Smallmouth bass, rock bass, redbreast sunfish, shad, river herring, striped bass, white perch, American eel, and all species of trout.

Directions: From Baltimore, take the Beltway (Interstate 695) to U.S. Highway 40 west to Marriottsville Road north. Follow Marriottsville Road to the parking lot on the left just past the railroad tracks and before the river, or continue on Marriottsville Road to the park entrance on the right.

DeLorme: Maryland and Delaware Atlas & Gazetteer: Page 57 B4, B5, and B6.

Accesses: Another access to the river is available in Sykesville off River Road.

In the Hollofield area, access can be had by taking Interstate 70 to U.S. Highway 29 south. Turn east on US 40; the entrance to the park is on the right just before crossing the Patapsco River. From Baltimore, take I-695 to US 40 west and travel approximately 2 miles; the entrance is just past the Patapsco River.

For the Avalon Area, take exit 47 from Interstate 95 onto Interstate 195. Continue on I-195 to exit 3, then take Maryland Highway 1 south to Elkridge. Turn right on U.S. Highway 1, heading south, then take the next right on South Street. The park entrance is on the left.

Description: Nearly 35 miles of the Patapsco River, from Woodbine in the west to Elkridge in the east, flows through Patapsco Valley State Park. Only a 1-mile stretch through Ellicott City lacks public access to the river from the park.

The Patapsco River averages about 50 feet in width. It is low in gradient, shallow, and rocky, with scattered deep pools and sandy runs. The many boulders provide pocket water that is excellent habitat for the stocked trout and smallmouth bass. The large, slow pools are also attractive to trout, bass, and sunfish.

The fishing: Smallmouth bass, rock bass, and redbreast sunfish are found throughout the river. In the early spring, anadromous species—gizzard, hickory, and American shad; river herring; striped bass; and white perch—migrate up the Patapsco. Gizzard shad and river herring can be seen swimming in the pool below Bloede Dam near the Denil fish ladder.

Bead-head nymphs, streamers resembling small herring, black gnats, and mosquito patterns work well for fly fishers targeting panfish and trout.

The Patapsco River is stocked with trout every year. It is managed as a put-and-take trout fishery (five trout per day) through nearly 10 miles of Patapsco Valley State Park. Rainbow trout up to 20 inches are released, and browns are occasionally stocked. This makes for excellent trout fishing from mid-October through early June. Water temperatures become too warm during the summer months to expect trout survival. The trout are stocked with the intention that all will be harvested by anglers before the Patapsco River becomes too warm for their survival.

The following areas are stocked with trout:

32a. The stocked area begins at Main Street in Sykesville (Carroll County) and West Friendship Road (Howard County) and extends downstream 6.5 miles to the confluence with the North Branch Patapsco River within the McKeldin Area of Patapsco Valley State Park.

32b. The lower section of put-and-take trout water is located northwest of US 1 in Elkridge within the Avalon Area of the state park. Trout are stocked from Bloede Dam downstream 3.5 miles to the B&O Viaduct.

32c. Another popular trout-fishing area on the Patapsco River is a 3.6-mile stretch from Daniels Dam downstream to Union Dam in the Hollofield Area of the park. This section was first stocked in 1995 and has a two-trout-per-day creel limit. With the reduced creel limit, more trout are available to anglers for a longer period of time than in the put-and-take sections. Spring and fall stockings provide great fishing for trout from October through early June. The Daniel's section has become very popular with fly anglers. Due to the river's large size through this section, there is plenty of room for casting a fly.

Restrictions: The put-and-take sections of the Patapsco River allow for a five-trout-per-day creel limit with no size or bait restrictions. There are two closure periods in the spring to allow for stocking, at which times no fishing is permitted within the designated put-and-take sections. There are no closure periods in the two-trout-per-day section of the river. The catch-and-return black bass section requires all bass to be immediately released to the water when caught. There are no bait restrictions; however, the Fisheries Service recommends not using bait, as higher bass mortality occurs with deep-hooked fish than with artificial lures and flies. Consult the *Maryland Freshwater Sportfishing Guide* for details on all license requirements as well as trout and black bass regulations associated with the Patapsco River.

Camping: Patapsco Valley State Park offers camping and many other amenities at the following areas: Hilton, Avalon, Glen Artney, Hollofield, Pickall, and McKeldin.

For more information: Patapsco Valley State Park; Maryland Department of Natural Resources, Fisheries Service, Central Region Office.

33 Piney Run Lake

Key species: Largemouth bass, crappie, striped bass, yellow perch, channel catfish, bluegill, redear sunfish, brown bullhead, tiger muskie, and rainbow trout.

Directions: From Baltimore, take the Beltway (Interstate 695) to exit 18, Maryland

Piney Run Lake boasts one of the best warm-water fisheries in Maryland.

Highway 26 (Liberty Road) west. Pass Maryland Highway 32 and take a left on White Rock Road, then take another left on Martz Road to the park entrance.

From Washington, take the Capitol Beltway (Interstate 495) to exit 31, Maryland Highway 97 north. Turn right on MD 26 and head east toward Eldersburg. Take a right on White Rock Road, then turn left on Martz Road to the park entrance.

DeLorme: Maryland and Delaware Atlas & Gazetteer: Page 57 A4.

Description: This 300-acre lake was completed by the US Army Corps of Engineers in 1974. Its maximum depth reaches 50 feet, and water clarity can be defined as clear. Artificial structures have been placed in close relation to fishing piers. In recent years, there has been an overabundance of vegetation, hindering boating and fishing strategies during the summer and fall.

Two boat ramps are available for a fee. Boat rentals, including canoes and pedal boats, are available at the boat ramp, and night crawlers are sold during the park season. During the summer, the park offers fishing excursions on its 25-passenger pontoon boat for a reasonable fee, where a guide takes you to the best fishing locations. A number of fishing tournaments are held at the park throughout the year, which include some night-fishing opportunities. Floating piers and fishing platforms provide additional angling possibilities.

The fishing: Piney Run Reservoir is one of the best warm-water fisheries in Maryland. Largemouth bass, redear sunfish, bluegill, yellow perch, channel catfish, and black crappie all grow to prodigious sizes. Naturally reproducing stripers afford anglers the opportunity to catch a really big fish, upwards of 30 pounds. Stocked tiger muskie have grown to over 36 inches. Rainbow trout are stocked annually in the lake.

Restrictions: Fishing is allowed only on approved shoreline and piers; no fishing from the dam structure, wildlife management area, or any steep embankment. Ice fishing and swimming are prohibited. Boats may only be launched from the two available boat ramps. Gasoline motors are prohibited. Boats are not permitted in the wildlife management area off White Rock Road.

The park hours are 6:00 a.m. to sunset daily April through October. During the off-season (November through March), parking is permitted outside the entrance gate from sunrise to sunset. Boats are not allowed on the lake during that time, and fishing is permitted from the shoreline only.

For more information: Piney Run Park; Maryland Department of Natural Resources, Fisheries Service, Lewistown Work Center.

34 Liberty Lake

Key species: Largemouth bass, smallmouth bass, bluegill, crappie, white perch, yellow perch, walleye, striped bass, brown and rainbow trout, channel catfish, and carp.

Directions: From Baltimore, take the Beltway (Interstate 695) to Maryland Highway 26 (Liberty Road) west to a right (north) on Oakland Mills Road, off of which two boat ramps are available.

DeLorme: Maryland and Delaware Atlas & Gazetteer: Page 57 A5.

Description: This lake covers 3,100 acres and is formed by an impoundment on the North Branch of the Patapsco River. Other tributaries include Beaver Run, Keyer's Run, Prugh Run, Morgan Run, Locust Run, and Cooks Branch. The reservoir is about 11 miles long, with a shoreline length at full pool of about 75 miles. The average depth is 59 feet, with a maximum depth of 144 feet.

The fishing: This reservoir is both a warm-water and cold-water fishery. Largemouth bass, smallmouth bass, bluegill, crappie, and white perch are the most popular warm-water fish. White crappie and bass often reach trophy-size. White perch still average about 10 inches despite being very plentiful in the reservoir.

Stocked striped bass now reproduce naturally, and they can run up to 40 pounds plus. Liberty Lake also supports a fine walleye fishery, sustained by good natural reproduction. A 12-pound walleye was surveyed recently.

White crappie and bass often reach trophy-size in Liberty Lake.

Restrictions: Boat propulsion is limited to rowing, paddling, or battery-powered motors. Fishing from a boat is allowed March 1 to December 31. A seasonal permit issued by the City of Baltimore Reservoir Natural Resources Office is required prior to launching a boat in Liberty Reservoir.

Regulations are complicated here, so check for current information on open areas and legal fishing methods.

Due to the potential for zebra mussel infestations, boaters on Liberty, Loch Raven, and Prettyboy Reservoirs must sign an affidavit stating their boat will be used only on these reservoirs. Live bait is prohibited unless purchased from a Maryland-certified zebra mussel–free bait store.

For complete regulations on fishing in Baltimore's reservoirs, go to the City of Baltimore Reservoir Natural Resources Office Web site.

For more information: Maryland Department of Natural Resources, Fisheries Service, Rivers and Reservoirs Project; City of Baltimore Reservoir Natural Resources Office.

35 Prettyboy Reservoir

Key species: Largemouth bass, smallmouth bass, crappie, channel catfish, yellow perch, and bluegill.

Directions: From Baltimore, take the Beltway (Interstate 695) to Interstate 83 north and exit on Maryland Highway 137 (Mount Carmel Road) west. Turn right (north) on Prettyboy Dam Road and follow it across the dam (the name of the road will change to Spooks Hill Road) to the launch area on the left.

DeLorme: Maryland and Delaware Atlas & Gazetteer: Page 75 B4.

Description: The Prettyboy watershed is one of the three area reservoir watersheds for the city of Baltimore. It is about 10 miles long and located in the northwest corner of Baltimore County. The lake covers about 1,600 acres, and the watershed is large, about 24,000 acres. It extends from the southern reaches of York County, Pennsylvania, and the northeastern corner of Carroll County, Maryland, into the northwestern corner of Baltimore County, where it drains into Prettyboy Reservoir. The municipalities of Hampstead and Manchester make up the western edge of the watershed.

The fishing: Prettyboy is a typical large, Middle Atlantic, warm-water fishery.

This reservoir is an excellent place to catch citation-size smallmouth and large-mouth bass. Crawdads are an excellent bait. Use an extra-sharp hook, 1-1/0 tied to line no heavier than 8-pound test. Squeeze a small split shot onto the line about 6 inches above the hook, and hook the crustacean through the tail. Fish the drop-offs and sunken structure.

Fly fishing is popular here for both panfish and bass. Try bream busters, mosquito and gnat patterns, popping bugs, and colorful streamers.

Restrictions: Boat fishing is allowed March 1 to December 31; gasoline engines are prohibited. No fishing from steep banks, rock cliffs, or other dangerous locations; at designated fish refuge areas; within 1,500 feet of Prettyboy Dam; or from bridges except in designated areas. The use of float tubes, chest waders, or hip boots is prohibited.

Live aquatic bait is prohibited unless purchased from a Maryland-certified zebra mussel–free bait store. Anglers using live bait must possess a receipt less than 48 hours old from the certified bait store where the bait was purchased. This prohibition applies to all live aquatic bait, including fish that have been caught in the reservoirs. Due to the potential for zebra mussel infestations, boaters on Liberty, Loch Raven, and Prettyboy Reservoirs must sign an affidavit stating their boat will be used only on these reservoirs.

For complete regulations on fishing in Baltimore's reservoirs, go to the City of Baltimore Reservoir Natural Resources Office Web site.

For more information: Maryland Department of Natural Resources, Fisheries Service, Rivers and Reservoirs Project; Prettyboy Watershed Alliance; City of Baltimore Reservoir Natural Resources Office; Prettyboy Reservoir Watershed Manager, (410) 887-5683 or sstewart@co.ba.md.us.

36 Gunpowder Falls

Key species: Brown trout, rainbow trout, and brook trout.

Directions: From Baltimore, take the Beltway (Interstate 695) to Interstate 83 north to exit 27, Mount Carmel Road. Turn right (east) on Mount Carmel Road, and at the traffic light, turn left (north) on York Road. Just past Hereford High School, turn left on Bunker Hill Road and follow it to the parking lot above the river. Other parking areas are located at Falls Road, Masemore Road, York Road, Big Falls Road, Blue Mount Road, Monkton Road, Glencoe Road, Sparks Road, and Phoenix Road.

DeLorme: Maryland and Delaware Atlas & Gazetteer: Page 75 B4.

Description: This stream ranges from 30 to 70 feet in width. The area above Falls Road has lots of deep pools and a moderate gradient. Below the falls, the river has a low gradient with deep pools, long runs, and swift cobble- and gravel-filled riffles.

From Corbett Road upstream to Blue Mount Road, the tailwater is wider and has many deep pools and gravel riffles. The extreme downstream section is slow and wide, with scattered pools and logs.

The first 0.4 mile of the Gunpowder Falls tailwater from Prettyboy Dam downstream flows through the City of Baltimore watershed property. The Gunpowder Falls State Park Hereford Area surrounds the next 6.6 miles of river. Much of the remaining tailwater flows through private property. Although most of the tailwater is accessible through the private property, please be aware of all private property signs and do not trespass where posted.

Hiking trails parallel the tailwater from Prettyboy Dam downstream to Big Falls Road. A hiking/biking trail parallels most of the tailwater from Blue Mount Road downstream to Phoenix.

The fishing: Brown trout overwhelmingly dominate in the upper areas of the Gunpowder Falls tailwater. They comprise 97 percent of the fishery, with brookies and rainbows making up the balance. Rainbows are mostly found between the dam and Falls Road. Brook trout are located throughout the stream, usually near the tributaries that hold them. Wild brown trout can be caught throughout the entire tailwater, however, with highest numbers existing upstream of the put-and-take section.

This is one of the most productive trout streams in Maryland. Biologists have measured adult brown trout from 56 pounds per acre to 109 pounds per acre in the catch-and-release section, an average of more than 2,000 per mile. Most of these are in the 8- to 11-inch range, but some are over 15 inches.

Rainbow trout grow faster than browns, and fish over 12 inches are common. The Maryland Department of Natural Resources is taking steps to increase the number of rainbows, because in some areas of Gunpowder their reproductive rates are poor.

This location is perfect for fly fishing. Most fly fishers prefer natural-looking bugs like mosquitoes and gnats, but colorful patterns are effective at times. Some anglers use streamers and other wet flies successfully.

Restrictions: This waterway is managed in three ways: catch-and-return, statewide wild trout, and put-and-take. Be sure to consult the *Maryland Freshwater Sportfishing Guide* for current details of where the boundaries of each of these areas are located.

For more information: Maryland Department of Natural Resources, Fisheries Service, Rivers and Reservoirs Project.

37 Loch Raven Reservoir

Key species: Largemouth bass, smallmouth bass, crappie, bluegill and other sunfish, chain pickerel, northern pike, channel and other catfish, yellow perch, white perch, and carp.

Directions: From Baltimore, take the Beltway (Interstate 695) to Interstate 83 north and exit at Timonium Road east. Follow Timonium Road to Dulaney Valley Road and turn left (north). Follow the road to a bridge over the reservoir.

DeLorme: Maryland and Delaware Atlas & Gazetteer: Page 75 D5.

Description: Loch Raven covers about 2,400 acres, and the watershed is 4,500 acres. The average depth is about 24 feet, and the shoreline runs for 38 miles. The reservoir is part of the water supply for the city of Baltimore.

The fishing: Loch Raven is considered the finest largemouth bass water in the state, and many 5-pound-plus fish are caught each year. Smallmouths also do well here, with fish over 5 pounds common.

Crappie, white perch, and bluegill are also plentiful and grow to good sizes. In addition, some very big channel cats are caught each year.

Restrictions: Boat propulsion is limited to rowing, paddling, or battery-powered motors. A seasonal permit issued by the City of Baltimore Reservoir Natural Resources Office is required prior to launching a boat in Loch Raven Reservoir. All boats must be at least 12 feet long with a 4-foot beam, and at least 18 inches deep. Boat fishing is allowed April 1 to November 27.

No fishing from steep banks, rock cliffs, or other dangerous locations; at designated fish refuge areas; or from bridges, except at designated platforms on the Dulaney Valley Road Bridge at Loch Raven. The use of float tubes, chest waders, or hip boots is prohibited.

Live aquatic bait is prohibited unless purchased from a Maryland-certified zebra mussel–free bait store. Anglers using live bait must possess a receipt less than 48 hours old from the certified bait store where the bait was purchased. This prohibition applies to all live aquatic bait, including fish that have been caught in the reservoirs. Due to the potential for zebra mussel infestations, boaters on Liberty, Loch Raven, and Prettyboy Reservoirs must sign an affidavit stating their boat will be used only on these reservoirs.

For complete regulations on fishing in Baltimore's reservoirs, go to the City of Baltimore Reservoir Natural Resources Office Web site.

For more information: Maryland Department of Natural Resources, Fisheries Service, Rivers and Reservoirs Project; City of Baltimore Reservoir Natural Resources Office; Baltimore County Department of Recreation and Parks; Loch Raven Fishing Center, 12101 Dulaney Valley Road, Towson, MD 21204; (410) 887-3871.

38 Deer Creek–Rocks State Park

Key species: Smallmouth bass, largemouth bass, brown trout, and rainbow trout.

Directions: From Baltimore, take the Beltway (Interstate 695) to U.S. Highway 1 north toward Bel Air, then take Maryland Highway 24 north to Rocks State Park.

DeLorme: Maryland and Delaware Atlas & Gazetteer: Page 76 B1.

Description: Deer Creek averages about 50 feet in width and contains excellent habitat for the stocked trout. Upper Deer Creek is a low-gradient stream. It is quite shallow, with rocky riffles and runs and scattered deep pools. The creek upstream of Rocks–Chrome Hill Road is unlike any other area in Rocks State Park. Running along MD 24, big boulders and falls of 10 to 12 feet abound here. This creates whitewater rapids resembling those at Great Falls on the Potomac River. This is a scenic view of Deer Creek you don't want to miss.

The fishing: Rainbow trout ranging from 9 to 20 inches raised at the Albert Powell State Fish Hatchery in Hagerstown are stocked into Deer Creek within the put-and-take trout management areas. Browns from private hatcheries are stocked occasionally to provide another species of trout for the angler to catch.

The put-and-take trout fishing areas are located within the Hidden Valley Natural Area of Rocks State Park and Harford County park property at Eden Mill. Upper Deer Creek within the Hidden Valley Natural Area and Eden Mill has been stocked with hatchery trout for more than 30 years and is a very popular put-and-take trout fishery in the spring. Fall stockings of hatchery fish increase the angling season for trout from October into early June. Deer Creek becomes too warm during the summer months for year-round trout survival.

Smallmouth bass are found throughout Deer Creek in low numbers. The lack of good adult habitat and the "flashy" nature of flows and high sediment input in the creek during storms, especially during the spring spawning period, appear to be the main limiting factors for the smallmouth population. The bass are small in size, as is typical in most small river systems, but an occasional large one can be found in the deeper pools.

Restrictions: The put-and-take trout areas of Deer Creek allow for a five-trout-per-day creel limit with no size or bait restrictions. There are two closure periods in the spring to allow for stocking. During the closures, fishing is not permitted within the designated put-and-take section from 1 mile south of Rocks State Park upstream to the bridge at Maryland Highway 23.

The closed season for all black bass (largemouth and smallmouth) in Maryland freshwater is March 1 through June 15. Anglers are allowed to catch and release bass during the closed season. There are no bait restrictions; however, the Fisheries Service recommends not using bait, as higher bass mortality occurs with deep-hooked fish than with artificial lures and flies.

Camping: There is no camping at Rocks State Park.

For more information: Rocks State Park; Maryland Department of Natural Resources, Fisheries Service, Central Region Office.

39 Deer Creek–Susquehanna State Park

Key species: Hickory shad, smallmouth bass, striped bass, and herring.

Directions: From Baltimore, take the Beltway (Interstate 695) to Interstate 95 north. Take exit 89 to Maryland Highway 155 east, then turn left (north) on Lapidum Road and follow it to the Susquehanna River. The road makes a hard left turn and becomes Stafford Road. Follow Stafford Road along the Susquehanna to the Stafford Road Bridge and the mouth of Deer Creek.

DeLorme: Maryland and Delaware Atlas & Gazetteer: Page 77 B4.

Description: Deer Creek has historically supported spawning runs of many species of anadromous fish. Hickory shad, white and yellow perch, and alewife and blueback herring all ran up the river, but then a private dam built on the creek at Wilson's Mill blocked approximately 25 miles of these fishes' spawning habitat. In 2000 a Denil fish ladder was built to reopen fish-spawning habitat in Deer Creek. Now all the species that had spawned in the creek in the past are doing so again.

The lower creek around Susquehanna State Park is low in gradient, with rocky riffles, sandy runs, and scattered sandy pools. The large, slow pools and runs are attractive resting areas for the spring migratory hickory shad and river herring.

A good ramp is located at the park's Lapidum Boating Facility. It offers direct access to Deer Creek and the Susquehanna River, and the headwaters of Chesapeake Bay are just a short trip downstream. The ramp is open year-round, and there is a fee. Yearlong passes are available and can be purchased at the park.

The fishing: The popular hickory shad and river herring fishery is within Susquehanna Park near the mouth of Deer Creek. From late March through early May, lower Deer Creek is a popular fishing destination, as thousands of river herring and hickory shad run up the creek to spawn. Anglers who come with an ultralight or light-action rod and a variety of shad darts and small jigs can hook into numerous hard-fighting shad. The Stafford Road Bridge area is a very popular destination for fly fishers, who come prepared with brightly colored streamers to entice the shad into taking their bait. Due to the popularity of the spring shad run, lower Deer Creek can get quite crowded, and with limited parking, an early start may be needed to get in on the action.

Smallmouth bass are found throughout Deer Creek in low numbers. The lack of good adult habitat and the "flashy" nature of flows and high sediment input in

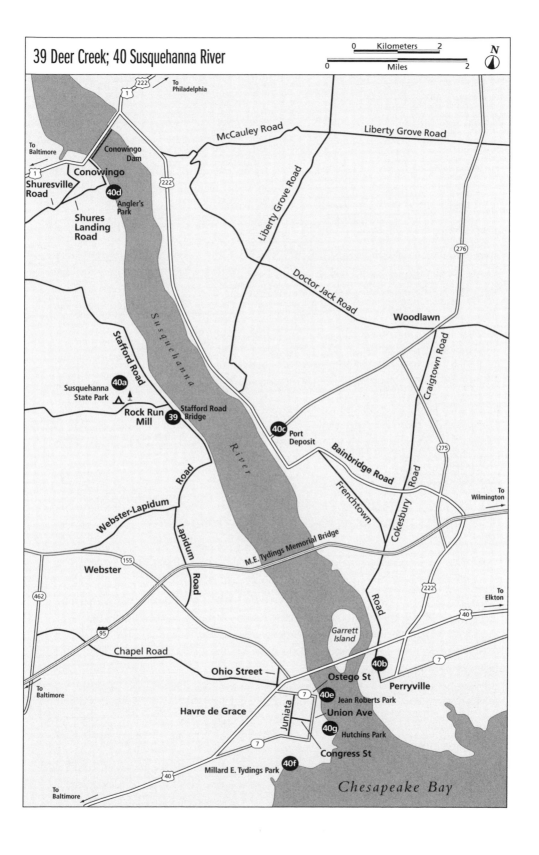

0   Kilometers   2

0   Miles   2

N

222
1
To Philadelphia

McCauley Road

Liberty Grove Road

To Baltimore

Conowingo Dam

Conowingo

1

222

Shuresville Road

40d

Angler's Park

Shures Landing Road

Liberty Grove Road

276

Doctor Jack Road

Woodlawn

Susquehanna

Stafford Road

Susquehanna State Park

40a

Rock Run Mill

39

Stafford Road Bridge

River

40c

Port Deposit

Bainbridge Road

Craigtown Road

275

Frenchtown

Cokesbury Road

To Wilmington

Road

Webster-Lapidum

Lapidum Road

155

Webster

462

M.E. Tydings Memorial Bridge

222

To Elkton

40

95

Chapel Road

Garrett Island

Road

To Baltimore

Ohio Street

Havre de Grace

Juniata

7

40b

Ostego St

Perryville

7

40e

Jean Roberts Park

Union Ave

40g

Hutchins Park

7

Congress St

40

Millard E. Tydings Park

40f

7

To Baltimore

Chesapeake Bay

the creek during storms, especially during the spring spawning period, appear to be the main limiting factors for the smallmouth population. The bass are small in size, as is typical in most small river systems, but an occasional large one can be found in the deeper pools.

Restrictions: There is a statewide moratorium on the harvest of American and hickory shad in Maryland. Catch-and-release fishing is permitted for shad. The season for alewife and blueback herring is January 1 through June 5, and there is no size or creel limit for the two river herring species. Please consult the *Maryland Freshwater Sportfishing Guide* for details on all license requirements as well as trout, black bass, herring, and shad regulations associated with Deer Creek.

The closed season for all black bass (largemouth and smallmouth) in Maryland freshwater is March 1 through June 15. Anglers are allowed to catch and release bass during the closed season. There are no bait restrictions; however, the Fisheries Service recommends not using bait, as higher bass mortality occurs with deep-hooked fish than with artificial lures and flies.

Camping: The Susquehanna State Park campground contains two loops with a total of 69 sites (6 of which have electric hookups), along with six camper cabins. Each loop has its own comfort station with hot showers. The campground is open May through September. Pets are welcome but must be leashed at all times. Reservations are highly recommended for weekend camping. Senior citizen discounts are applicable Sunday through Thursday.

For more information: Susquehanna State Park; Maryland Department of Natural Resources, Fisheries Service, Central Region Office.

40 Susquehanna River

Key species: Largemouth bass, walleye, white perch, hickory shad, striped bass, blueback herring, smallmouth bass, channel and other catfish, and bluegill.

Directions: From Baltimore, take the Beltway (Interstate 695) to Interstate 95 north. The interstate crosses the Susquehanna at the M. E. Tydings Bridge near Havre de Grace.

DeLorme: Maryland and Delaware Atlas & Gazetteer: Page 77 B4 and C4.

Accesses: **40a, Susquehanna State Park.** A good ramp is located at the park's Lapidum Boating Facility, offering direct access to Deer Creek and the Susquehanna River. The headwaters of Chesapeake Bay are just a short trip downstream. The ramp is open year-round, and there is a fee. Yearlong passes are available and can be purchased at the park. Fishing piers are also available at the park. To get there, take I-95 to Maryland Highway 155 south. Turn left (north) on Lapidum Road. This ends at the ramp.

40b, Perryville. A nice boat ramp can be found at Perryville. A permit is required. From I-95 exit on Maryland Highway 275 south. Turn right (south) onU.S. Highway 222 to a right (west) on U.S. Highway 40. Follow signs to the river.

40c, Port Deposit. A nice ramp and seawall are located in Port Deposit on the north bank of the river. A permit from the town is required. From Baltimore, take the Beltway (I-695) to I-95 north. After crossing the M. E. Tydings Memorial Bridge over the Susquehanna, pick up MD 275 north at exit 93. At Craigtown, turn left (west) on Bainbridge Road (US 222). At Port Deposit, the road makes a sharp right. The ramp and seawall are located in the park on the left (west) side of the road, just after the turn.

40d, Conowingo Dam. This tremendous dam is located toward the end of the Susquehanna. Lots of shore fishing is available under the dam at Angler's Park, and launching a canoe or kayak is also possible. From Baltimore, take the Beltway (I-695) to U.S. Highway 1 north. Before the dam, make a right (south) on Shuresville Road. At Shures Landing Road, make a very sharp left (east) and follow it to the end. A fishing area with parking is available.

40e, Havre de Grace–Jean Roberts Park. A nice public boat ramp (fee) can be found here. From Baltimore, take the Beltway (I-695) to I-95 north. Before the M. E. Tydings Memorial Bridge, take exit 89 to MD 155 south. Turn right (south) on Ohio Street, then left (east) on Ostego Street and follow it to the water. The ramp is located almost under the railroad trestle.

40f, Havre de Grace–Millard E. Tydings Park. Another nice ramp (fee) is located in this park. From Baltimore, take the Beltway (I-695) to I-95 north. Before the M. E. Tydings Memorial Bridge, take exit 89 to MD 155 south. Turn right (south) on Ohio Street, then left (east) on Ostego Street. Make a right (south) on Union Avenue and follow it to the park.

40g, Havre de Grace–Hutchins Park. A fishing pier is located at this park. From Baltimore, take the Beltway (I-695) to I-95 north. Before the M. E. Tydings Memorial Bridge, take exit 89 to MD 155 south. Turn right (south) on Ohio Street, then left (east) on Ostego Street. Make a right (south) on Union Street, then turn left (east) on Congress Street and drive to the water.

Description: This is the largest drainage into Chesapeake Bay.

The fishing: Both anadromous and freshwater fish are found in the Susquehanna River. It presents tidal fishing opportunities in the spring, when river herring and white and hickory shad move into the river and Deer Creek for spawning. The shad fishing is catch-and-release only.

A large white perch run also occurs in the spring. White perch are catch-and-keep. The Susquehanna River is a great place to find smallmouth bass, which can be caught year-round but kept only during open season. Rockfish can also be kept when in season. Walleye and catfish also inhabit the river.

The Susquehanna Flats are famous for striped bass. The depths run from just a couple feet to 20 feet, and the area covers many dozens of square miles. It's a popular fishing spot in the spring.

Caution: Water levels rise rapidly from the discharge from Conowingo Dam. The rocks can be slippery, so be careful when wading. They can also damage boats.

Restrictions: A Chesapeake Bay Sport Fishing License is required for ages 16 and over. Check the current *Maryland Tidal Sportfishing Guide* for creel limits, sizes, and seasons. Pay particular attention to the striped bass regulations.

Hickory and white shad are catch-and-release only.

Camping: The Susquehanna State Park campground contains two loops with a total of 69 sites (6 of which have electric hookups), along with six camper cabins. Each loop has its own comfort station with hot showers. The campground is open May through September. Pets are welcome but must be leashed at all times. Reservations are highly recommended for weekend camping. Senior citizen discounts are applicable Sunday through Thursday.

For more information: Susquehanna State Park; Perryville Town Hall; Havre de Grace City Yacht Basin; Havre de Grace Office of Tourism & Visitor Center; Maryland Department of Natural Resources, Fisheries Service, Central Region Office; tide information, http://tbone.biol.sc.edu/tide/tideshow.cgi?site=Havre+de+Grace, +Susquehanna+River,+Maryland&glen=7.

41 Rising Sun Pond

Key species: Largemouth bass, crappie, bluegill, pumpkinseed, carp, and stocked trout.

Directions: From Baltimore, take the Beltway (Interstate 695) to Interstate 95 north. Take exit 93 to Maryland Highway 275 north (Craigtown Road), then make a right on Maryland Highway 276 north (Jacob Tome Memorial Highway). Turn right on Maryland Highway 273 east (Rising Sun Road); the pond will be on the left (north) side of road before you enter the town of Rising Sun.

DeLorme: Maryland and Delaware Atlas & Gazetteer: Page 77 A5.

Description: Rising Sun Pond is 1 acre in size and has a maximum depth of 11 feet. The shallow areas are covered with a rooted aquatic vegetation called elodea. This plant makes excellent cover for fish to live in; however, it is hard to control and can be a nuisance. Each spring a special dye is applied to the pond to control the elodea. This dye is biodegradable and is not harmful to fish or humans.

There are four benches near the pond where people may sit and fish. This is a nice place to spend a leisurely afternoon fishing and picnicking with the kids.

The fishing: Rising Sun Pond is a standard bass/bluegill lake and is managed as such. Good numbers and sizes of these fish are present. Anglers should be prepared to use weedless lures to fish around the aquatic vegetation. Other species can be caught, including white and black crappie, pumpkinseed, common carp, and stocked trout during the spring.

Restrictions: Gas motors are prohibited; electric trolling motors are recommended. Camping and swimming are not allowed.

Trout are stocked each spring to allow for a special provision where only children under the age of 16, persons 65 and older, and the legally blind can fish between March 1 and May 15. On May 16, the pond returns to limited harvest with no age restrictions.

For more information: Maryland Department of Natural Resources, Wildlife & Heritage Service, Bel Air Regional Office; Maryland Department of Natural Resources, Fisheries Service, Eastern Region Office.

Southern Maryland

This chapter covers Charles, Calvert, and St. Mary's Counties and portions of Prince George and Anne Arundel Counties. The region provides excellent Chesapeake angling for striped bass and other salty species as well as some great bass and crappie lakes. The Patuxent River runs through the center of the area and provides some of the finest river angling in Maryland.

42 Potomac River/Mattawoman Creek–Smallwood State Park

Key species: Largemouth bass, smallmouth bass, various catfish, bluegill, white perch, yellow perch, carp, and crappie.

Directions: From Washington, take the Capitol Beltway (Interstate 495) to Maryland Highway 210 south (Indian Head Highway). Take Maryland Highway 225 east in Indian Head, then make a right (west) on Maryland Highway 224 and follow the signs to the Smallwood State Park entrance on your right.

To reach the Mattingly Park ramp, take MD 210 south from I-495 into the town of Indian Head, then make a left (south) on Mattingly Avenue just before the base gates. The ramp is at the end of the road.

DeLorme: Maryland and Delaware Atlas & Gazetteer: Page 36 D2.

Description: Though Mattawoman Creek is a shallow tributary of the Potomac River, it does have a defined channel for most of its navigable length. A 6 mph speed limit, which is enforced by the military, applies on the north side of the creek. Vegetation can be thick during the summer, and lily pads abound. Other good fishing structures include downed trees, overhanging brush, concrete riprap, old barges, and pilings.

At Mattingly Park, a small pier is available for fishing, but there is only limited shore access. Inquire at the park office as to areas open to fishing. The boat launch is best suited for small bass boats or similar watercraft, and a launch fee applies.

Several piers located at Sweden Point Marina are open to fishing. The marina has accommodations for large boats and six boat ramps (fees apply). Small boat rentals are also available, along with restrooms, showers, laundry facilities, and a small store with dock-side fuel (gas, no diesel), ice, bait and tackle, firewood, snacks, and souvenirs.

The fishing: Largemouth bass is the most sought-after species, but Mattawoman also has catfish, carp, bluegill and pumpkinseed sunfish, perch, pickerel, crappie, and longnose gar. An occasional striper is not out of the question either.

Restrictions: A Chesapeake Bay Sport Fishing License is required to fish the tidal portion of Mattawoman Creek and the tidal Potomac. The dividing line for Mattawoman Creek is MD 225. Above the bridge a Freshwater Fishing License is

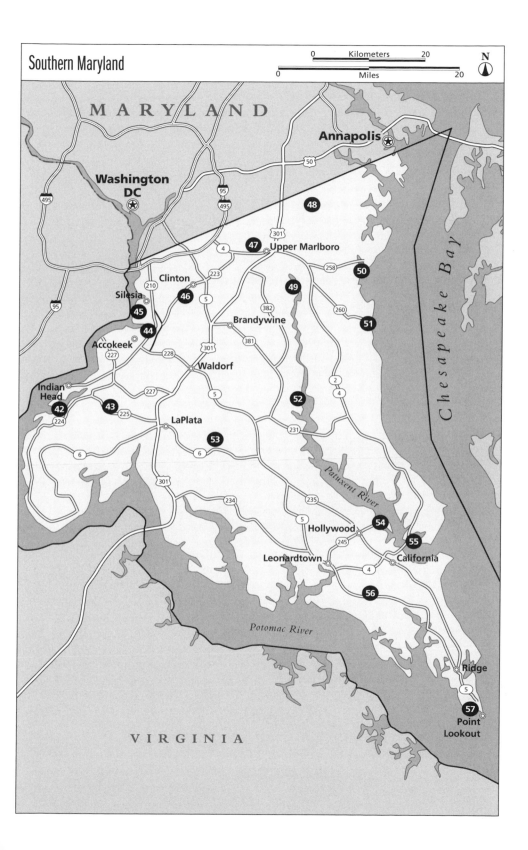

required. Always check with the Maryland Department of Natural Resources for up-to-date regulations.

Camping and lodging: Smallwood State Park offers 15 family campsites with electric hookups under the canopy of a hardwood forest, each with a picnic table, lantern post, and fire ring. Bathhouse facilities with hot showers are also provided. In addition, there are four camper cabins that sleep four people and two cabins that sleep six, with heat and air-conditioning. Camping is seasonal, so contact the park for dates.

For more information: Smallwood State Park; Maryland Department of Natural Resources, Fisheries Service, Cedarville Visitor's Center; tide information, www.dnr.state.md.us/fisheries/access/tide_finder.html.

43 Myrtle Grove Lake and Greentree Reservoir

Key species: Largemouth bass, bluegill, pickerel, catfish, and stocked trout.

Directions: From Washington, take the Capitol Beltway (Interstate 495) to Maryland Highway 210 south (Indian Head Highway). At Bryans Road, go south on Maryland Highway 227 to Maryland Highway 224 south to Bumpy Oak Road

Myrtle Grove offers year-round fishing and easy access.

south. At Marshalls Corner, turn right (west) on Maryland Highway 225. Pass Ripley and take the dirt road on the right (north) to the Myrtle Grove Wildlife Management Area. The lake is at the end of the road.

DeLorme: Maryland and Delaware Atlas & Gazetteer: Page 36 D3.

Description: Both the 23-acre Myrtle Grove Lake and the 10-acre Greentree Reservoir are located within the Myrtle Grove Wildlife Management Area.

The fishing: Both lakes yield bountiful harvests of largemouth bass, bluegill, pickerel, and catfish. Here, anglers will find year-round fishing and easy access. Trout are stocked in Myrtle Grove Lake on a seasonal basis.

For more information: Maryland Department of Natural Resources, Fisheries Service, Cedarville Visitor's Center.

44 Piscataway (National) Park

Key species: Largemouth bass, smallmouth bass, catfish, bluegill, white perch, yellow perch, carp, and crappie.

Directions: From Washington, take the Capitol Beltway (Interstate 495) to Maryland Highway 210 south (Indian Head Highway). After passing Farmington Road, take a right at the next stoplight onto Livingston Road (look for B&J Carryout). Drive 1 block and turn right on Biddle Road. At the stop sign, turn left on Bryan Point Road, follow it to the end, and make a right into the parking lot.

DeLorme: Maryland and Delaware Atlas & Gazetteer: Pages 36 B3 and 37 B4.

Description: Piscataway Park is truly a beautiful place. Wildlife abounds, with bald eagles, beavers, deer, foxes, ospreys, and many other species observed regularly. Visitors can stroll on two boardwalks over freshwater tidal wetlands. A number of nature trails, meadows, and woodland areas offer an educational experience for the entire family.

The fishing: Some bank fishing is available at Piscataway Park at Farmington Landing and the National Colonial Farm. Farmington Landing is on the south side of the park and can be reached via Wharf Road. National Colonial Farm is located just south of Piscataway Park and is on the main stem of the Potomac. A fishing pier is available at Piscataway Park. Information as to places to fish can be obtained at the park visitor center.

Restrictions: A Chesapeake Bay Sport Fishing License is required to fish the tidal portion of Piscataway Creek and the tidal Potomac. On Piscataway Creek, the dividing line between fresh and tidal waters is the bridge on Maryland Highway 224 (Livingston Road). Above the bridge a Maryland Freshwater Fishing License is required. Check with the Maryland Department of Natural Resources for current regulations.

Piscataway (National) Park; Maryland Department of Natural Resources, Fisheries Service, Cedarville Visitor's Center; tide information, www.dnr.state.md.us/fisheries/access/tide_finder.html.

45 Potomac River–Piscataway Creek to Fort Washington (National) Park

Key species: Largemouth bass, smallmouth bass, catfish, bluegill, white perch, yellow perch, carp, and crappie.

Directions: For Fort Washington Park, from Washington take the Capitol Beltway (Interstate 495) to Maryland Highway 210 south (Indian Head Highway). In Silesia, turn right (west) on Fort Washington Road and follow it to the park.

To reach the Fort Washington Marina, take MD 210 south to Fort Washington Road and go right (west) to Warburton Drive south. Turn south on King Charles Terrace and follow the road to the marina.

DeLorme: Maryland and Delaware Atlas & Gazetteer: Page 37 B4.

Description: The park covers 341 acres and has picnic areas, hiking and biking trails, and playgrounds for the kids. There is a fee for entering the park, but annual passes can also be purchased.

Fort Washington Marina gives boating access (fee) to Piscataway Creek and the Potomac. Boats and kayaks are available for rent. The marina also has a restroom and some vending machines.

The fishing: Deep water can be found off the point and off Fort Washington Park, while shallow water dominates the area above and below the lighthouse. For erosion prevention, the point has been riprapped with boulders. Much of the creek itself is very shallow, so follow the markers carefully. However, some of the best fishing is around the docks and wharfs at the shoreline, so it is worth trying to find your way through the flats. Fish the grass beds for bass and perch and the deeper holes for monster catfish.

Shore-bound anglers can fish at the base of the lighthouse where Piscataway Creek meets the Potomac River.

Restrictions: A Chesapeake Bay Sport Fishing License is required to fish the tidal portion of Piscataway Creek and the tidal Potomac. On Piscataway Creek, the dividing line between fresh and tidal waters is the bridge on Maryland Highway 224 (Livingston Road). Above the bridge a Maryland Freshwater Fishing License is required. Check with the Maryland Department of Natural Resources for current regulations.

For more information: Fort Washington (National) Park; Fort Washington Marina; Maryland Department of Natural Resources, Fisheries Service, Cedarville Visitor's Center; tide information: www.dnr.state.md.us/fisheries/access/tide_finder.html.

46 Cosca Lake

Key species: Largemouth bass, crappie, bluegill, redear sunfish, and rainbow trout.

Directions: From Baltimore, take the Beltway (Interstate 695) to Interstate 97 south. Exit at Maryland Highway 3 south, which becomes U.S. Highway 301 near Bowie. Continue south on US 301 and turn right (west) on Maryland Highway 4 in Upper Marlboro. Turn left (south) on Maryland Highway 223 (Woodyard Road), pass through Clinton, and turn left (south) on Brandywine Road. Take the right fork, Thrift Road, and follow it to Cosca Regional Park. The lake is on the right.

From Washington, take the Capitol Beltway (Interstate 495) to Maryland Highway 5 south. Follow MD 5 to Jenkins Corner and turn right (south) on Old Branch Avenue, which becomes Brandywine Road. Take the right fork, Thrift Road, and follow it to Cosca Regional Park. The lake is on the right.

DeLorme: Maryland and Delaware Atlas & Gazetteer: Page 37 B5.

Description: Cosca Lake covers 11 acres and is located in Cosca Regional Park in Clinton. Besides fishing, the park offers lots of outdoors activities. The Clearwater Nature Center is a must-see for visitors. Boats are available for rent at the park.

A trail circumnavigates Cosca Lake, making the entire shoreline accessible to anglers.

The fishing: A trail circumnavigates the lake, making the entire shoreline accessible to anglers. Nice largemouth bass and big crappie, bluegill, redear, and stocked rainbow trout make fishing here interesting. The lake can become weedy during the summer and difficult to fish.

Camping: The park has 25 campsites, some with water and electric hookups.

For more information: Cosca Regional Park; Maryland Department of Natural Resources, Wildlife & Heritage Service, Prince Frederick Office.

47 Schoolhouse Pond

Key species: Largemouth bass, crappie, bluegill, and rainbow trout.

Directions: From Washington, take U.S. Highway 50 east and exit at U.S. Highway 301. Go south on US 301 to a right (west) on Old Marlboro Pike at Upper Marlboro, then make a right (north) on Governor Oden Bowie Drive. The lake is on the right side of the road.

From Baltimore, take the Beltway (Interstate 695) to Interstate 97 south. Exit at Maryland Highway 3 south, which becomes US 301 near Bowie, and continue south. Turn right (west) on Old Marlboro Pike at Upper Marlboro, then make a right (north) on Governor Oden Bowie Drive. The lake is on the right side of the road.

DeLorme: Maryland and Delaware Atlas & Gazetteer: Page 47 D6.

Description: This pond is right in downtown Upper Marlboro. Parking is on the street, though it might be difficult finding a space during the week.

The fishing: It would probably be difficult to launch a boat into this pond unless you know a landowner; however, a nice barrier-free pier is available. Fishing here is surprisingly good, with bass up to 16 inches and crappie up to 10 inches taken.

For more information: Maryland Department of Natural Resources, Wildlife & Heritage Service, Prince Frederick Office.

48 Middle Patuxent River–Queen Anne Fishing Area and Canoe Launch

Key species: Largemouth bass, striped bass, American eel, bluegill, redbreast sunfish, pumpkinseed, carp, chain pickerel, and warmouth.

Directions: From Washington, take the Capitol Beltway (Interstate 495) to U.S. Highway 50 east. Turn south on U.S. Highway 301 near Bowie, then turn left (east) on Queen Anne Bridge Road and proceed to the park entrance. Turn left at the entrance to the Patuxent River 4-H Center and take the gravel road to the landing. Access is restricted.

From Baltimore, take the Beltway (Interstate 695) to Interstate 97 south. Exit at Maryland Highway 3 south, which becomes US 301 near Bowie, and continue south. Turn left (east) on Queen Anne Bridge Road and follow the directions above.

DeLorme: Maryland and Delaware Atlas & Gazetteer: Page 48 C1

Description: The middle Patuxent River is a slow-flowing lowland stream that runs right through the center of the Southern Maryland section. It is very scenic, with numerous backwaters, and is pleasant to float.

The Queen Anne Fishing Area is open daily except during winter. Anglers are permitted on the old bridge and along both sides of the river. A floating pier is located next to the canoe launch, which is a launch site for the Patuxent River Water Trail. Flooding is common, so check river conditions before heading out.

The fishing: The species in this river are of the typical Middle Atlantic warm-water riverine variety. Five-pound largemouth bass are caught on a regular basis, and good-size chain pickerel readily hit spoons and other lures. Carp fishing is also good, and many anglers fish for them with dough balls or corn from the piers or banks.

Restrictions: A special-use permit or reservation, available through the Queen Anne Fishing Area, is required for all activities. The river is tidal, so a Chesapeake Bay Sport Fishing License is required for anglers 16 and older. Check current regulations with the Maryland Department of Natural Resources.

For more information: Queen Anne Fishing Area and Canoe Launch.

49 Patuxent River State Park

Key species: Largemouth bass, pickerel, bluegill, redbreast sunfish, pumpkinseed, American eel, carp, and warmouth.

Directions: From Washington, take the Capital Beltway (Interstate 495) to exit 11A (Pennsylvania Avenue) and Maryland Highway 4 east. Turn right on U.S. Highway 301 south, then turn left (south) on Croom Station Road. Turn left (east) on Croom Road (Maryland Highway 382), then left (east) again on Croom Airport Road. At the park entrance, either continue straight to the Group Camp Area or turn left and proceed 1.7 miles to the park office.

From Baltimore, take the Beltway (Interstate 695) to Interstate 97 south. Exit at Maryland Highway 3 south, which becomes US 301 near Bowie. Follow US 301 south, then turn left (south) on Croom Station Road and follow directions above.

DeLorme: Maryland and Delaware Atlas & Gazetteer: Page 38 A1, B1, and C1; Page 48 D1.

Accesses: **49a, Selby's Landing.** Follow Croom Airport Road (past the park entrance road) to the dead end, turn left, and follow the road to the designated area. Parking is limited to 25 vehicles, including those with trailers.

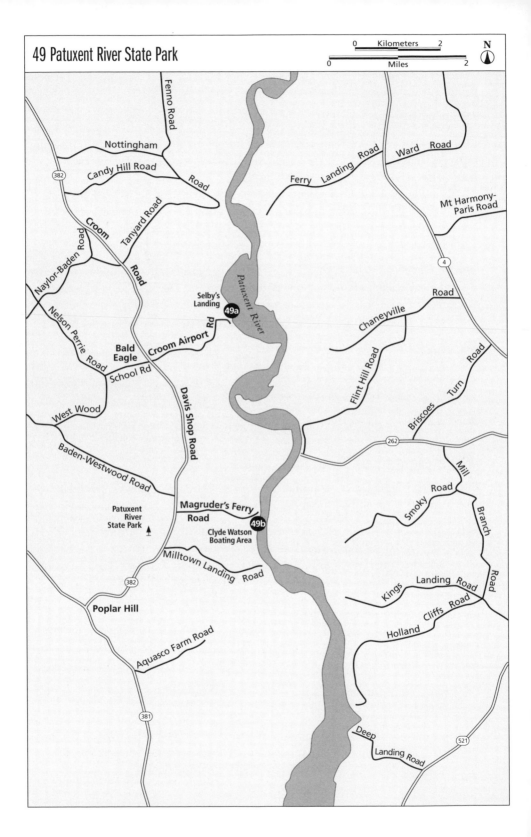

Kilometers

Miles

N

Fenno Road

Nottingham Road

Candy Hill Road

382

Croom Road

Tanyard Road

Naylor-Baden Road

Nelson Perrie Road

Selby's Landing

49a

Patuxent River

Ferry Landing Road

Ward Road

Mt Harmony-Paris Road

4

Road

Chaneyville

Flint Hill Road

Briscoes Turn Road

Bald Eagle School Rd

Croom Airport Rd

West Wood

Baden-Westwood Road

Davis Shop Road

Patuxent River State Park

Magruder's Ferry Road

49b

Clyde Watson Boating Area

262

Smoky Road

Mill Road

Branch Road

382

Milltown Landing Road

Poplar Hill

Kings Landing Road

Holland Cliffs Road

Aquasco Farm Road

381

Deep Landing Road

521

49b, Clyde Watson Boating Area. Follow Croom Road south past Croom Airport Road, at which point the name changes to Davis Shop Road. Turn left (east) on Magruder's Ferry Road and go 1.2 miles to the park entrance on the right. Parking is limited to 15 vehicles with trailers plus 25 additional vehicles.

Description: This portion of the 6,700-acre Patuxent River State Park is located in Prince George County. In addition to fishing, recreational uses include hunting, hiking, and horseback riding. Paths are unmarked. A portion of the park is a state wildlands area.

The park periodically holds a Hey! Let's Go Fishing Day. This fun program, held at an 8-acre catch-and-release bass pond, is for beginners and equipment is provided; a fee applies. Children must be accompanied by an adult.

The fishing: This park has a number of fishing accesses, and the angling is about the same in all the areas. Bass are the primary target, but excellent panfishing can also be had. Some anglers fish for carp with dough balls and canned corn.

For more information: Patuxent River State Park.

50 Deale

Key species: Striped bass, cobia, Spanish mackerel, croaker, spot, bluefish, red drum, black drum, flounder, speckled trout, gray trout, and white perch.

Directions: From Washington, take the Capitol Beltway (Interstate 495) to Maryland Highway 4 east. Continue on MD 4 to Bristol, then pick up Maryland Highway 258 east and follow it to Deale.

From Baltimore, take the Beltway (Interstate 695) to Interstate 97 south and exit at Maryland Highway 3 south, which becomes U.S. Highway 301 near Bowie. Follow US 301 south to MD 4 east near Upper Marlboro. Continue on MD 4 to Bristol, then pick up MD 258 east and follow it to Deale.

DeLorme: Maryland and Delaware Atlas & Gazetteer: Page 38 A3.

Description: Deale is a quaint fishing village, and most amenities are available. The town is located right on the shores of Chesapeake Bay, and fishing is the primary concern of almost all who visit or live there.

A boat ramp is available in Deale but has limited parking. Turn into Shipwright Harbor for access. Another boat ramp is available at JJ's Tackle Shop.

The fishing: All the Chesapeake Bay species are caught out of Deale. Striped bass (rockfish) is the most popular, but bluefish and gamesters are also taken. Bottom-bouncing for croaker, spot, trout, and flounder is also popular.

A large charter fleet is available for excursions; see the appendix. A productive pier located next to JJ's Tackle Shop on Rockhold Creek Road provides angling opportunities for shore-bound fishers. Surf casting off the beach is also possible.

For more information: Annapolis and Anne Arundel County Chamber of Commerce.

51 Chesapeake Beach

Key species: Striped bass, cobia, Spanish mackerel, croaker, spot, bluefish, red drum, black drum, flounder, speckled trout, gray trout, and white perch.

Directions: From Washington, take the Capitol Beltway (Interstate 495) to Maryland Highway 4 east. Continue on MD 4 past Lyons Creek, then turn left (east) on Maryland Highway 260 and follow it to Chesapeake Beach.

From Baltimore, take the Beltway (Interstate 695) to Interstate 97 south and exit at Maryland Highway 3 south, which becomes U.S. Highway 301 near Bowie. Follow US 301 south to MD 4 east near Upper Marlboro. Continue on MD 4 past Lyons Creek, then turn left (east) on MD 260 and follow it to Chesapeake Beach.

DeLorme: Maryland and Delaware Atlas & Gazetteer: Page 38 B3.

Description: Chesapeake Beach is a very tourist-oriented area, with every amenity imaginable available. The city is located right on the beaches of Chesapeake Bay.

A fine boat ramp is located at Breezy Point Marina. Launch fees apply.

This nice spadefish was caught by the author off Chesapeake Beach.

The fishing: All the Chesapeake Bay species are caught out of Chesapeake Beach. Striped bass (rockfish) is the most popular, but bluefish and gamesters are also taken. Bottom-bouncing for croaker, spot, trout, and flounder is also popular.

A large charter fleet is available for excursions, and a productive pier provides angling opportunities for shore-bound fishers. Surf casting off the beach is also possible.

For more information: Calvert County Chamber of Commerce.

52 Middle Patuxent River–Cedarhaven Fishing Area

Key species: Bluegill, largemouth bass, catfish, black crappie, pickerel, stocked trout, shad, chub, carp, sucker, striped bass, and yellow perch.

Directions: From Washington, take the Capitol Beltway (Interstate 495) to Maryland Highway 5 south. Turn south on U.S. Highway 301 near Brandywine, then take Short Cut Road east. Turn right (east) on Brandywine Road, then go south on Maryland Highway 381. Turn left (east) on Eagle Harbor Road, then bear left on Trueman Point Road and left again on Banneker Boulevard. The park entrance is straight ahead.

From Baltimore, take the Beltway (Interstate 695) to Interstate 97 south and exit at Maryland Highway 3 south, which becomes US 301 near Bowie. Follow US 301 south past Upper Marlboro, then turn left (east) on Maryland Highway 382 (Croom Road) and left (south) again on MD 381. After a few miles, turn left (east) on Eagle Harbor Road, then bear left on Trueman Point Road and left again on Banneker Boulevard. The park entrance is straight ahead.

DeLorme: Maryland and Delaware Atlas & Gazetteer: Page 38 D1.

Description: The Patuxent River is over a mile wide at the Cedarhaven Fishing Area, which is located near the town of Eagle Harbor in the southeastern corner of the county.

The fishing: A T-shaped pier is provided for anglers, and many also fish along the shoreline. Long casts may be necessary, so surf rods are recommended.

Restrictions: A special-use permit or reservation is required for all activities, and a Chesapeake Bay Sport Fishing License is also required.

For more information: Cedar Haven Fishing Area.

53 Wheatley Lake, also known as Gilbert Run

Key species: Channel catfish, largemouth bass, black crappie, redear sunfish, bluegill, and stocked rainbow trout.

Directions: From Washington, take the Capitol Beltway (Interstate 495) to Maryland Highway 5 south past Waldorf. Near Bryantown, turn right (south) on Oliver Shop Road, then turn left on Maryland Highway 6 (LaPlata–New Market Road) and enter Gilbert Run Park on the left (north).

From Baltimore, take the Beltway (Interstate 695) to Interstate 97 south and exit at Maryland Highway 3 south, which becomes U.S. Highway 301 near Bowie. Continue south on US 301 through Waldorf to LaPlata. In LaPlata, turn left on MD 6 (LaPlata–New Market Road) and follow it east approximately 6 miles to the Gilbert Run Park entrance on the left.

DeLorme: Maryland and Delaware Atlas & Gazetteer: Page 29 A5.

Description: The Charles County Department of Recreation owns Gilbert Run Park, in which Wheatley Lake is found. This impoundment was completed in the 1970s and covers 60 acres. A boat ramp is available, along with fishing supplies and licenses and concessions. Gilbert Run Park is open from March through November, with seasonal hours of operation. Be sure to take a look at the 150-gallon fish tank in the park's nature center.

The fishing: Wheatley Lake is relatively shallow, with the deepest section near the dam. Submerged aquatic vegetation can be a problem, especially in the summer if you are fishing the shoreline areas. However, the lake holds excellent populations and is definitely worth fishing.

Restrictions: No gasoline engines. Check with the Maryland Department of Natural Resources for current regulations.

For more information: Gilbert Run Park; Charles County Department of Public Facilities; Maryland Department of Natural Resources, Fisheries Service, Cedarville Visitor's Center.

54 Greenwell State Park

Key species: Striped bass, croaker, spot, white perch, catfish, and bluefish.

Directions: From Washington, take the Beltway (Interstate 495) to Maryland Highway 210 south. Near Accokeek, turn left (east) onto Maryland Highway 373 (Accokeek Road), then right (south) onto Bealle Hill Road. Turn left (east) on Maryland Highway 228, then pick up Maryland Highway 5 south in Waldorf. Follow MD 5 to the junction of Maryland Highway 235 south near Harpers Corners. In Hollywood, turn left (east) on Maryland Highway 245 (Sotterley Gate Road) and travel 2.5 miles. Make a right (east) on Steerhorn Neck Road; the park entrance is the second drive on the left in approximately 0.8 mile.

From Baltimore, take the Beltway (Interstate 695) to Interstate 97 south. Take the U.S. Highway 50 exit east to Maryland Highway 2 south, which eventually joins up with Maryland Highway 4. Near Solomons, MD 4 and MD 2 separate. Take MD 4 south across the Governor Johnson Memorial Bridge, then in California turn right (north) on MD 235 toward Hollywood. Turn right (east) on MD 245 (Sotterley Gate Road) and travel 2.5 miles. Make a right (east) on Steerhorn Neck Road; the park entrance is the second drive on the left in approximately 0.8 mile.

DeLorme: Maryland and Delaware Atlas & Gazetteer: Page 30 B3.

Description: Primarily created as a hiking and equestrian park, Greenwell is a 596-acre state park located on the Patuxent River. In 1971 John Phillip Greenwell Jr. and his sister, Mary Wallace Greenwell, donated their 166-acre farm to the state of Maryland for public use. The state subsequently purchased the adjacent 430-acre property and joined the two to form the existing park.

The fishing: Visitors may fish from the pier or from the revetment year-round.

Restrictions: A Chesapeake Bay Sport Fishing License is required in tidewaters and a Freshwater Fishing License is required in nontidal waters. Licenses are required for persons age 16 and older.

For more information: Greenwell State Park.

55 Patuxent Saltwater-Solomons

Key species: Striped bass, hardhead, cobia, black drum, red drum, Spanish mackerel, spot, gray trout, speckled trout, flounder, and bluefish.

Directions: From Washington, take the Capitol Beltway (Interstate 495) to Maryland Highway 4 south. This eventually merges with Maryland Highway 2. Continue on MD 4/2, and when the roads separate, follow MD 2 to Solomons.

From Baltimore, take the Beltway (Interstate 695) to Interstate 97 south. Take the U.S. Highway 50 exit east to MD 2 south. Follow MD 2, which eventually joins up with MD 4, all the way to Solomons.

DeLorme: Maryland and Delaware Atlas & Gazetteer: Page 31 C4.

Description: Located at the mouth of the Patuxent River, Solomons offers fishing in both Chesapeake Bay and the river. In addition, the city is located relatively close to the mouth of the Potomac River, so the charter fleet can take advantage of that fishery. The season runs from April through December.

A boat ramp can be found at the base of the Governor Johnson Memorial Bridge.

The fishing: Both bottom fishing and trolling are popular in this area. Bottom-bouncers will often hook up with multiple species in a day. A lot of charter boat fishing comes out of Solomons. The Pepper Langley Fishing Pier is a popular hangout for shore-based anglers.

Restrictions: A Chesapeake Bay Sport Fishing License is required.

For more information: St. Mary's County Chamber of Commerce.

56 St. Mary's River State Park

Key species: Largemouth bass, bluegill, crappie, redear sunfish, and pickerel.

Directions: From Washington, take the Beltway (Interstate 495) to Maryland Highway 210 south. Near Accokeek, turn left (east) onto Maryland Highway 373 (Accokeek Road), then right (south) onto Bealle Hill Road. Turn left (east) on Maryland Highway 228. In Waldorf, take Maryland Highway 5 south and continue through Chingville, then turn left (north) on Camp Cosoma Road and follow it to the lake.

From Baltimore, take the Beltway (Interstate 695) to Interstate 97 south. Get off at Maryland Highway 3 south, which becomes U.S. Highway 301 near Bowie. In Waldorf, take MD 5 south and continue through Chingville, then turn left (north) on Camp Cosoma Road and follow it to the lake.

DeLorme: Maryland and Delaware Atlas & Gazetteer: Page 30 C3.

Description: St. Mary's River State Park is separated into two areas, Site 1 and Site 2. Site 1 holds the 250-acre St. Mary's Lake. Located along MD 5, between Leonardtown and Great Mills at the end of Camp Cosoma Road, the area has become a popular freshwater fishing spot. A nice boat launch is available here.

The fishing: St. Mary's Lake has been designated a trophy bass lake, and as such, special fishing regulations may be in effect. In addition to bass, crappie up to 2 pounds and bluegill up to 10 inches are relatively common. Many anglers come here to catch chain pickerel that run up to 30 inches. Weedless spoons and other lures are very effective.

Fly fishers can have loads of fun with the panfish and bass. Use small wet or dry flies for the 'gill and large hairy bugs for the bucketmouths.

Anglers should check bulletin boards or contact park personnel for fishing details. A 7.5-mile trail circles the lake, allowing it to be fished from the shore in addition to boat.

Restrictions: This is a designated trophy largemouth bass lake, so be sure you know all the current regulations. Gasoline engines are not allowed, but electric motors are legal.

For more information: St. Mary's River State Park.

57 Point Lookout State Park

Key species: Hardhead, bluefish, rockfish, spot, flounder, gray trout, and speckled trout.

Directions: From Baltimore, take the Beltway (Interstate 695) to Interstate 97 south to Maryland Highway 3 south, which turns into U.S. Highway 301 near Bowie. Follow US 301 south to Maryland Highway 4 south in Upper Marlboro and take MD 4 all the way across the bridge. After the bridge, at the first traffic light, turn left on Maryland Highway 235 south and follow it into Ridge to a blinking red traffic light. Turn left on Maryland Highway 5 south and follow it as far as it goes to Point Lookout. After the entrance sign, take the second road on the right to the campground. At the campground, park on the left side of the road and register at the ranger station.

From Washington, take the Beltway (Interstate 495) to the Maryland Highway 4/Pennsylvania Avenue exit. Take MD 4 south to Upper Marlboro, then follow directions above from Upper Marlboro to the campground.

DeLorme: Maryland and Delaware Atlas & Gazetteer: Page 23 B3.

Description: Point Lookout is a peninsula formed by the confluence of Chesapeake Bay and the Potomac. It is ideally located so that anglers can head up the Potomac or farther up the bay. Many family-oriented activities are available in addition to fishing, making it a great place to spend a weekend or extended vacation.

A fish-cleaning station is available at the boat launch area. The park also has four launch ramps, 97 pull-through parking spaces, and boat slips (fee). Point Lookout Concession rents 16-foot John Dories and canoes. Boats go quickly, so arrive early. Food, beverages, and fishing supplies are also available.

The fishing: The pier at Point Lookout State Park juts out 710 feet into Chesapeake Bay. During the hot summer months, the salinity changes, allowing the middle bay's fish to be caught from the pier. Fishing is also allowed along the entire length of the causeway. Large riprap boulders line some of the shoreline. Lake Conoy is also available for fishing and offers a wide variety of species.

Camping and lodging: There are 143 wooded campsites available; some have full hookups, some only have electric, and others are dry. A campsite for youth groups is also available. Please contact the park for hours and closures in advance of your visit.

The park also offers cottage and cabin rentals. The cottage sleeps six and has a bathroom and a fully equipped kitchen. A two-night minimum stay is required April and October; weekly rentals only May through September (closed November through March). Each of the six cabins sleeps four and includes a full-size bed, a set of bunk beds, heat/air-conditioning, picnic table, fire ring, and grill. The minimum stay restrictions do not apply to the cabins.

For more information: Point Lookout State Park.

Eastern Shore of Maryland

The Eastern Shore of Maryland has some of the best saltwater, brackish, and freshwater fishing available anywhere along the east coast of the United States. Because of the area's unique geographical and demographic characteristics, angling opportunities abound. This chapter covers Wicomico, Dorchester, Kent, Queen Anne's, Talbot, Caroline, Somerset, and Worchester Counties and part of Cecil County.

Maryland's Eastern Shore is part of a peninsula with the Atlantic Ocean on one side and Chesapeake Bay on the other. In some places it is only a short drive from the ocean to the bay. Because of this, saltwater anglers can choose where to fish depending on what they wish to catch and where the run is the strongest at any particular time. It is also convenient when the wind velocities are high. If winds are out of the easterly quarter, the bayside is calmer than the seaside. During periods of west winds, the opposite is true.

Though changing, the Eastern Shore is still quite rural. As such, fishing pressure is less than in more populated areas, making for more satisfying experiences. Boat ramps are abundant, and shore-fishing opportunities are numerous. Most boat ramps are public, built and maintained by the state or the individual counties or municipalities, and many of them have associated piers and docks. At times there is excellent shore-based fishing from these structures.

Saltwater fishing on the Eastern Shore of Maryland (and the Delaware ocean areas, too) is a year-round activity. Starting in the winter—some years as early as January, depending on how cold it is—tautog remain active over the offshore wrecks, reefs, and rock piles. Anglers travel from as far as Boston and even Florida to participate in this run.

By the end of March, when the water temperatures reach about 45 to 50 degrees, tautog become active over inshore areas such as rock piles and wrecks. Bulkheads, jetties, and bridge pilings become possible angling areas. Early in the season, fish the bottom on the ebb tide, as the constricted waters of the back bays warm much faster than the ocean.

By late April, the first run of croaker begins to show up bayside. These fish do not bite as soon as they arrive, but the netters start taking them in the more restrictive bodies of water adjacent to the bay. One of the first areas where anglers get a shot at hardheads is in Pocomoke Sound.

After the croaker appear bayside, a few gray trout (weakfish) start showing up in the catch. This usually occurs in late April and continues through June. Some years there are so many trout that lots of anglers actually target this species. Also mixed in with the croaker and trout are a few small to medium bluefish, along with an occasional tackle buster.

Most years, flounder fishing in the seaside bays like Assawoman, behind the Ocean City barrier islands, begins sometime in May and June. Early in the season, fish the restricted waters, which are usually warmer this time of year. Also during this time, the spring striped bass (rockfish) season begins in Chesapeake Bay. This is mostly a trophy season, as many large bruisers are taken.

Black drum, the poor man's small-boat big game, also begin to show up in May. They run up the Chesapeake, while those bound for Delaware Bay swim along the seaside. These guys can tip the scales anywhere from 10 pounds to as high as 80 or 90 pounds. Fishing for drum is usually good through much of June. Big ones may be found almost anywhere, but fishing depths between 8 and 40 feet appears to be best. Some specific areas are Hoopers Strait and the Targets (see Crisfield chapter).

By late May, the seaside black drum run is in full swing. While this is mostly a Delaware Bay fishery, occasionally drum may be taken around Ocean City and Indian River inlets. At times the fish are caught from the beach on Assateague Island or Ocean City.

By mid-June, the waters off the Eastern Shore begin to settle into the typical summer fishery; that is, a variety of fish. Some flounder will still be available on both sides as well as croaker, speckled trout, gray trout, and some whiting. As the waters warm, some porgy, triggerfish, pigfish (grunts), pinfish, and a few sheepshead begin to show up in the catch.

Sea bass and some porgy begin to take over the rock piles and wrecks, replacing tautog. These fish are usually available through November. This is primarily a seaside activity, and though plenty are caught in the Chesapeake, most are undersized.

This is also the time that cobia begin their annual run, mostly in the Virginia part of the lower bay. However, enough are taken in Maryland waters for anglers to take note. If the summer is quite warm, on the seaside a few cobia will venture as far north as Delaware Bay. These guys could run upward of 80 pounds. Spadefish is another summer species that gets a lot of attention in Virginia, but many make it into Maryland. This fishery is mostly in Chesapeake Bay, but many of the offshore wrecks and buoys on the seaside also are havens for spadies.

Midsummer inshore fishing can be hit or miss depending on the year. However, persistent anglers can catch a respectable amount of varied species. Offshore, trollers and chunkers usually do well with various blue-water fish like tuna, bonita, king mackerel, wahoo, and marlin. Closer to home, some anglers pull various artificials to catch Spanish mackerel.

Usually in mid-September, the best fishing of the year begins and could last through the end of October or early November. On the seaside, all the species previously mentioned become very active as they prepare for their offshore and southerly migrations.

In October, the Chesapeake bayside sees its best run of flounder for the year. These are the largest flatfish caught in the waters off the shore. This run can last through December if it doesn't get too cold.

The tautog also become active in October. On the seaside, they are mixed with sea bass and become more and more prominent in the catch as the water cools. They

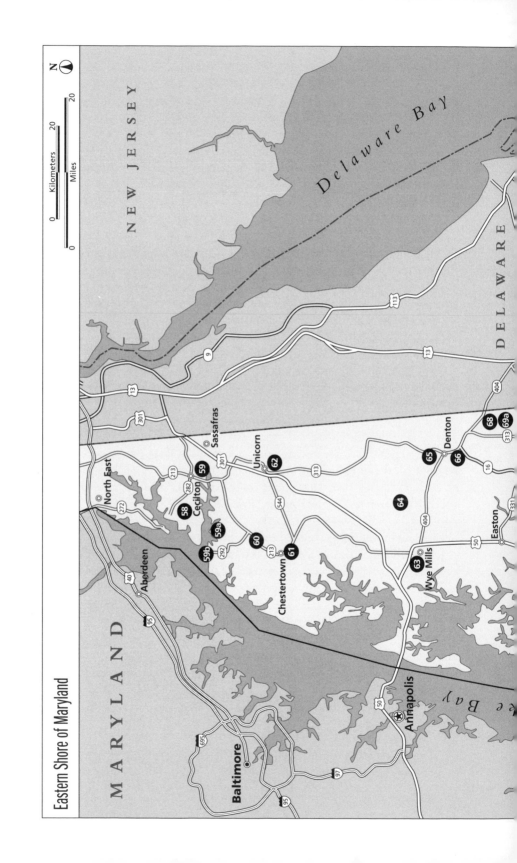
Eastern Shore of Maryland

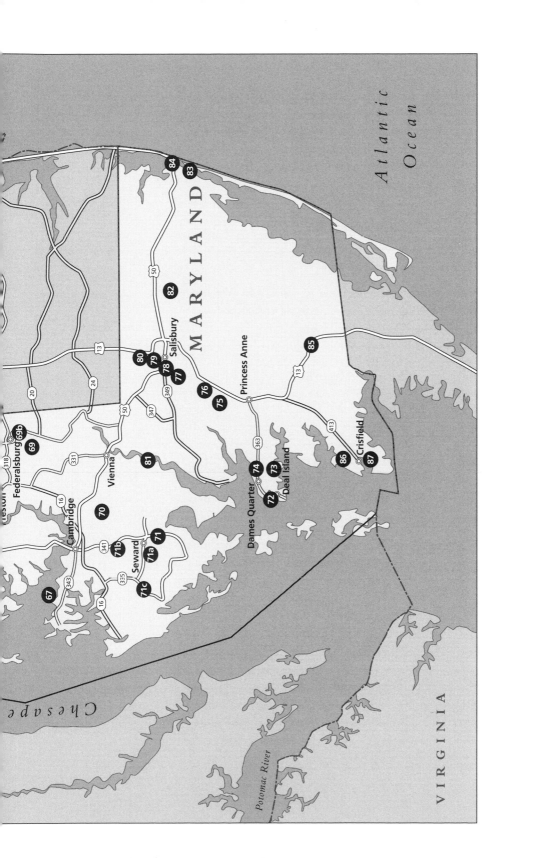

also start stirring in Chesapeake Bay. These guys keep biting through December in the bay and all winter off the seaside.

The striped bass season starts on the bayside in mid-October. The early fish are usually small throw-backs, but a few legal specimens will be mixed in. As the season progresses, larger rockfish move down the Chesapeake, and by late November that fishery is in full swing. The bay rockfish season ends by mid-December.

On the seaside, the first stripers usually show up in November and the season peaks in December. These fish can actually be caught all winter long. Most are at least legal-size, and some run up to 50 pounds.

58 Stemmers Run Reservoir

Key species: Largemouth bass, bluegill, crappie, carp, green sunfish, American eel, and channel catfish.

Directions: From Baltimore, take the Beltway (Interstate 695) to Interstate 95 north to Maryland Highway 272 south toward North East. Turn left (east) on U.S. Highway 40, then take a right (south) on Maryland Highway 213 to Cecilton and another right (west) on Maryland Highway 282 (Grove Neck Road). Veer right on Pond Neck Road, then make a right onto the gravel road that leads to the Elk River boat ramp (the turn is just before the paved road). Follow the gravel road, which parallels the Elk River, then make a right at the water diversion and follow the road to the primitive boat ramp.

From Annapolis, take U.S. Highway 50 east over the Bay Bridge, then take U.S. Highway 301 north. Make a left on Maryland Highway 313 (Galena Road), then take MD 213 north to Cecilton. Turn left (west) at the light on MD 282 (Crystal Beach Road), then turn left again on Grove Neck Road (still MD 282). Veer right on Pond Neck Road and follow the directions above.

DeLorme: Maryland and Delaware Atlas & Gazetteer: Page 60 A3.

Description: This broad, shallow, and turbid lake has a maximum depth of only 6 feet. A large part of the shoreline is covered with the exotic invasive species of reed called phragmites, which makes it a bit difficult to get down to the water in some places. Several fish structures have been placed over the past few years throughout the middle section of the reservoir. Stemmers Run is also managed for waterfowl hunting.

The fishing: Stemmers Run Reservoir is a standard bass/bluegill lake and is managed as such. Good numbers and sizes of these fish are present. Bass have abundant forage on which to feed and can be finicky as a result. Channel catfish have been stocked to help utilize all the forage. Anglers may occasionally catch other species including pumpkinseed, black crappie, white crappie, green sunfish, common carp, American eel, brown bullhead, golden shiner, gizzard shad, and spottail shiner.

Restrictions: A permit is required to fish the reservoir, which can be obtained by calling the Maryland Department of Natural Resources. Fishing is prohibited in all areas during waterfowl and firearm deer-hunting seasons, except Sundays. Camping and swimming are prohibited.

For more information: Maryland Department of Natural Resources, Fisheries Service, Eastern Region Office.

59 Sassafras River

Key species: Largemouth bass, striped bass, chain pickerel, crappie, channel and other catfish, bluegill and other sunfish, white perch, and yellow perch.

Directions: From Baltimore, take the Beltway (Interstate 695) to Interstate 97 south, then take U.S. Highway 50 east across the Bay Bridge. U.S. Highways 50 and 301 run together for a few miles; when they separate, continue on US 301 north, which crosses the Sassafras River near the town of Sassafras. The Sassafras Harbor Marina is on the east side of the north end of the bridge.

DeLorme: Maryland and Delaware Atlas & Gazetteer: Page 60 A2 and A3.

Accesses: **59a, Turner's Creek Park.** Follow the directions above to US 301 north. Take US 301 past Queenstown to Maryland Highway 213 north. Follow MD 213 to Kennedyville, then take Turner's Creek Road north to the park.

59b, Betterton Beach County Park. Follow the directions above to US 301 north. Take US 301 past Queenstown to MD 213 north. Before Kennedyville, turn (left) north on Still Pond Road (Maryland Highway 292) and follow it to the end at Betterton.

Description: The Sassafras River is very picturesque. Though it is primarily a Maryland stream, its headwaters are in western Delaware. The Sassafras forms the natural boundary between Kent and Cecil Counties in Maryland before it empties into the upper Chesapeake Bay.

A nice pier is available at Turner Creek Park for shore-bound anglers, along with plenty of opportunity for bank fishing. A good ramp is also found here.

Betterton Beach County Park is located near the mouth of the Sassafras. It has a stone jetty that can be fished as well as a transient boat ramp.

The fishing: For bass, try Lucky Craft crankbait, Senkos, buzzbaits, spinnerbaits, plastic frogs, and jigs when fishing deep. The Yamamoto IKA tube is particularly effective.

For more information: Sassafras River Association; Kent County Parks and Recreation (Turner's Creek and Betterton Beach Parks); Kent County Tourism Development Office; Maryland Department of Natural Resources, Fisheries Service, Eastern Region Office.

60 Urieville Community Lake

Key species: Largemouth bass, chain pickerel, crappie, bluegill and other sunfish, yellow perch, and white perch.

Directions: From Baltimore, take the Beltway (Interstate 695) to Interstate 97 south, then take U.S. Highway 50 east across the Bay Bridge. U.S. Highways 50 and 301 run together for a few miles; when they separate, continue on US 301 north. Take Maryland Highway 213 north and pass through Chestertown. Urieville Community Lake is on your left.

DeLorme: Maryland and Delaware Atlas & Gazetteer: Page 60 B2.

Description: Y-shaped Urieville Lake is about 35 acres in size, with an average depth of about 3 feet. The spillway below the dam in Morgan Creek creates a unique habitat and is a popular place for anglers during the spring fishing season.

The fishing: Urieville Lake supports a standard bass/bluegill fishery and is managed accordingly. Aquatic vegetation covers the lake during the summer months, making boating and fishing very difficult. Usually, the only open water in the summer is near the dam. Anglers may also occasionally catch other species, including pumpkinseed, brown bullhead, golden shiner, and common carp.

Restrictions: No horsepower limitation exists on this lake; however, the watercraft speed limit is 6 knots. Camping and swimming are not permitted.

For more information: Maryland Department of Natural Resources, Fisheries Service, Eastern Region Office.

61 Chester River

Key species: Striped bass, largemouth bass, crappie, a few species of catfish, herring, shad, bluegill and other sunfish, chain pickerel, white perch, and yellow perch.

Directions: From Baltimore, take the Beltway (Interstate 695) to Interstate 97 south, then take U.S. Highway 50 east across the Bay Bridge. U.S. Highways 50 and 301 run together for a few miles; when they separate, continue on US 301 north. Take Maryland Highway 213 north, which crosses the Chester River at Chestertown.

DeLorme: Maryland and Delaware Atlas & Gazetteer: Page 60 C2, C3, and D1; Page 49 A6 and B6; Page 50 A1; Page 59 D6.

Accesses: Much of the land along the Chester River is private; however, numerous accesses are available for anglers. The following are accesses to the lower river:

61a, Gray's Inn Landing. From MD 213 on the north end of Chestertown, take Maryland Highway 20 south to Rock Hall. Pick up Maryland Highway 445 south out of Rock Hall, then turn left (east) on Grays Inn Landing Road and proceed to the end of the road.

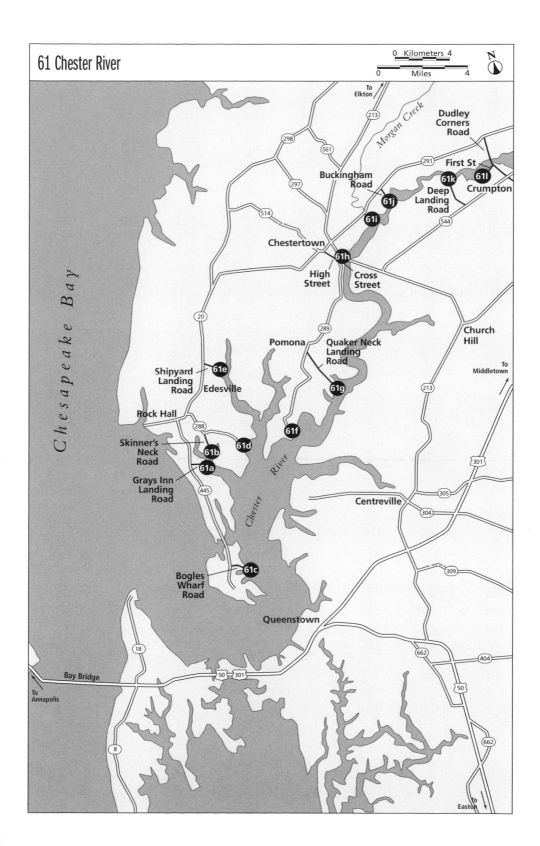

61 Chester River

0 Kilometers 4
0 Miles 4

N

To Elkton

Morgan Creek

213

298

561

291

Dudley Corners Road

First St

61k

61l

Crumpton

297

Buckingham Road

Deep Landing Road

61j

514

61i

544

Chestertown

61h

High Street

Cross Street

Church Hill

20

289

Pomona

Quaker Neck Landing Road

To Middletown

Shipyard Landing Road

61e

213

Edesville

61g

Rock Hall

288

61f

Skinner's Neck Road

61b

61d

301

Chester River

61a

305

Grays Inn Landing Road

445

Centreville

304

Chesapeake Bay

Chester River

309

61c

Bogles Wharf Road

Queenstown

18

662

404

Bay Bridge

50

301

50

To Annapolis

8

662

To Easton

61b, Skinner's Neck Ramp. Take MD 20 north out of Rock Hall to Maryland Highway 288 east. At the T, turn right (south) on Skinners Neck Road and follow it to the ramp on the left.

61c, Bogles Wharf Ramp. From MD 213 on the north end of Chestertown, take MD 20 south to Rock Hall. Pick up MD 445 south out of Rock Hall and follow it across the bridge to Eastern Neck Island. Continue on MD 445 to a left fork, which is Bogles Wharf Road, and take it to the end of the road.

61d, Long Cove Ramp. Take MD 20 north out of Rock Hall, then turn right (east) on MD 288 and follow it to the end, where the ramp is located.

61e, Shipyard Landing. Take MD 20 north out of Rock Hall through Edesville, then turn right (east) on Shipyard Landing Road and follow it to the ramp at the end of the road.

61f, Cliffs City Ramp. From Chestertown, take Maryland Highway 289 south and follow it to the end, where the ramp is located.

61g, Quaker Neck Landing. From Chestertown, take MD 289 south. Continue through Pomona, then turn left (south) on Quaker Neck Landing Road (Maryland Highway 661) and follow it to the ramp at the end of the road.

Here are three accesses near Chestertown:

61h, High Street Ramp. After crossing the river heading north on MD 213 in Chestertown, turn left (south) on Cross Street. Turn left (east) on High Street and follow it to the riverfront.

61i, Morgnec. At the north end of Chestertown, go east on Maryland Highway 291. The fishing area is found after crossing Morgan Creek. A canoe launch is located here.

61j, Buckingham Wharf. Continuing east on MD 291 beyond Morgnec, turn right (east) on Buckingham Road and follow it to the water.

The following two accesses are farther upriver:

61k, Deep Landing. From MD 213 before Chestertown, take Maryland Highway 544 east to McGinnes. Turn left (north) on Deep Landing Road and follow it to the boat ramp. Shore fishing is also possible here.

61l, Crumpton. Continue east on MD 544 to Dudley Corners Road (Maryland Highway 290) north. Make a left (west) on First Street in Crumpton and follow it to the ramp. Shore fishing is also possible here.

Description: This is another Eastern Shore lowland meandering river. Some of the shoreline is quite developed, but much of it is wooded or farmland. The river starts as a small stream near Unicorn and winds up being a mile wide at its mouth at Chesapeake Bay.

The fishing: Anglers can expect a mix of freshwater and anadromous species in this river. Large bass are taken upstream and, depending on the year, almost as far downstream as the mouth. Excellent white perch fishing is available, especially in the spring. Bluegill and catfish are relatively easy to catch.

For more information: Chester River Association; Maryland Department of Natural Resources, Fisheries Service, Eastern Region Office; tide information, www.free tidetables.com/tides/?tti=2869.

62 Unicorn Community Lake

Key species: Largemouth bass, bluegill, crappie, chain pickerel, American eel, channel catfish, brown bullhead, white perch, and yellow perch.

Directions: From Baltimore, take the Beltway (Interstate 695) to Interstate 97 south, then take U.S. Highway 50 east across the Bay Bridge. U.S. Highways 50 and 301

Nice largemouth bass like this can be taken from Unicorn Lake.

run together for a few miles; when they separate, continue on US 301 north. Take a right (east) on Maryland Highway 300 (Church Hill-Sudlerville Road), then turn left (north) on Maryland Highway 313 (Sudlersville-Millington Road). Take a right into the Unicorn Fish Hatchery; a boat ramp and small pier are located behind the office. No parking is behind the office, so park in front.

DeLorme: Maryland and Delaware Atlas & Gazetteer: Page 62 C4.

Description: This 43-acre impoundment is rather shallow, with a maximum depth of 8 feet and a mean depth of roughly 4 feet. Cool water is input year-round by the Unicorn Branch, which is the major tributary to the lake. Brown trout can survive in this creek throughout the year.

The shoreline of Unicorn Lake is mostly forested, lending to some woody debris in the lake, which is a preferred fish habitat. Evergreen tree fish attractors have been placed in the lower half of the lake near the dam. Aquatic vegetation proliferates during late spring and summer and can become a hindrance to angling.

Picnic tables and small shelters are available, along with a fine paved boat ramp and an ample bank-fishing area.

The fishing: Unicorn provides quality fishing for both largemouth bass and bluegill. Anglers may occasionally catch other species, including chain pickerel, pumpkinseed, green sunfish, channel catfish, brown bullhead, black crappie, yellow perch, white perch, American eel, and creek chubsucker. The Unicorn dam tailrace provides excellent spring fishing for bluegill, blueback herring, and white and yellow perch.

Restrictions: No horsepower limitation exists for the lake; however, the watercraft speed limit is 6 knots. Electric trolling motors are preferred. Swimming and camping are not permitted.

For more information: Maryland Department of Natural Resources, Fisheries Service, Eastern Region Office.

63 Wye Mills Community Lake

Key species: Largemouth bass, crappie, bluegill, chain pickerel, yellow perch, brown bullhead, carp, sucker, and pumpkinseed.

Directions: From Baltimore, take the Beltway (Interstate 695) to Interstate 97 south, then take U.S. Highway 50 east across the Bay Bridge. Continue on US 50 toward Easton and take a right (south) on Maryland Highway 213. The parking lot and boat ramp is on the left before the small bridge.

DeLorme: Maryland and Delaware Atlas & Gazetteer: Page 50 C2.

Description: Wye Mills Lake has a maximum depth of 8 feet while the average is 4 feet. At 50 acres, it is among the largest impoundments on the Eastern Shore. The upper part of the lake is shallow with gradual drop-offs. Steeper banks with sharp drop-offs are found from midlake to the lower end.

Many downed trees and undercut roots line the shore, providing excellent fish habitat. Aquatic vegetation could be a problem during the summer months. Fish attractors have been placed along the concrete dam and can be cast to from the bank.

The fishing: Good-size bass are relatively common in Wye Mills Lake, making it an excellent place to catch a big one. Because of the abundant forage, bass can be picky at times. Trophy bluegill are also caught.

Restrictions: There is no horsepower limitation for the lake; however, the watercraft speed limit is 6 knots. Electric trolling motors are preferred. Swimming and camping are not permitted.

For more information: Maryland Department of Natural Resources, Fisheries Service, Eastern Region Office.

64 Tuckahoe Lake

Key species: Largemouth bass, crappie, bluegill, chain pickerel, yellow perch, brown bullhead, carp, sucker, and pumpkinseed.

Directions: From Baltimore, take the Beltway (Interstate 695) to Interstate 97 south, then take U.S. Highway 50 east across the Bay Bridge. Turn left on Maryland Highway 404 east near Wye Mills, then turn left (north) on Maryland Highway 480 (Hillsboro-Ridgely Road). Take the first left (north) on Eveland Road, then turn left (west) on Crouse Mill Road and drive over both bridges. The parking lot and boat ramp are on your right.

DeLorme: Maryland and Delaware Atlas & Gazetteer: Page 50 C3.

Description: At 19 acres in size, Tuckahoe Lake is rather shallow. The maximum depth is 7 feet near the dam, and the average is about 6 feet. The lake has a rather flat, consistent bottom.

The fishing: Good fishing for both bass and bluegill can be had in Tuckahoe Lake. Besides these two species, fishing around stumps and roots can yield chain pickerel.

Stumps, roots, and undercut banks are characteristic of the upper portion of the lake, which is great habitat for bass, bluegill, and chain pickerel. The remainder of the lake has limited rooted aquatic vegetation near the shoreline.

Restrictions: Gas motors are prohibited, but electric trolling motors are allowed. Camping and swimming are prohibited.

For more information: Tuckahoe State Park; Maryland Department of Natural Resources, Fisheries Service, Eastern Region Office.

Choptank River

The Choptank River is a major tributary of Chesapeake Bay. The headwaters are located in Kent County, Delaware. It flows out of Mud Mill Pond and straddles the Delaware-Maryland border. The stream passes into Maryland permanently in Caroline County near Mount Moriah, Delaware. The Choptank courses through Caroline County and then forms much of the border between Talbot and Caroline Counties and Dorchester County. The mouth of the river is located south of Eastern Bay. The Choptank runs next to Denton, where it widens, and then Cambridge, where it is about a mile wide.

Since this fishery is so diverse, we have divided this river into three separate site descriptions: the Upper Choptank, Martinek State Park and the Lower Choptank.

65 Upper Choptank River

Key species: Largemouth bass, striped bass, white perch, yellow perch, chain pickerel, channel and other catfish, bluegill and other sunfish, and crappie.

The Upper Choptank River near Greensboro is a great place to chase largemouth bass and catfish.

Directions: The Upper Choptank can be reached from Baltimore by taking the Beltway (Interstate 695) to Interstate 97 south. In Annapolis, take U.S. Highway 50 east across the Bay Bridge. Continue on US 50 to Wye Mills, then take Maryland Highway 404 east to Denton, where the road crosses the river.

DeLorme: Maryland and Delaware Atlas & Gazetteer: Page 51 C4 and D4.

Accesses: **Greensboro Ramp.** In Wye Mills, take MD 404 east to Hillsboro, then take Maryland Highway 480 north to Greensboro. Turn right (east) on Maryland Highway 314 (Greensboro-Whiteleysburg Road). The ramp is located to the south off Sunset Avenue.

Denton Ramp. In Wye Mills, take MD 404 east through Hillsboro and turn south on MD Business 404 before crossing the river in Denton. After the bridge, look for signs to Daniel Crouse Park, which is on the left (north) side of the road. The ramp is in the park.

Description: Shore and dock fishing is available at the access points listed above. In Denton, Crouse Park's public landing is very popular with bass fishermen. It is close to the downtown area, which has stores, cafes, and restaurants. Shore fishing is good from the park.

The fishing: The Upper Choptank is a typical Middle Atlantic warm-water fishery. Largemouth bass is the primary target of most anglers. However, catfish is a close second, and there are some excellent specimens in the Choptank. Crappie, perch, and bluegill fishing is also good.

Restrictions: Be sure to check the current Maryland regulations for this area.

For more information: Caroline County Recreation & Parks.

66 Martinak State Park

Key species: Largemouth bass, striped bass, white perch, yellow perch, pickerel, channel and other catfish, bluegill, and crappie.

Directions: From Baltimore, take the Beltway (Interstate 695) to Interstate 97 south. In Annapolis, take U.S. Highway 50 east across the Bay Bridge. Continue on US 50 to Wye Mills, then take Maryland Highway 404 east through Hillsboro and cross the river into Denton. Continue south and east to a right (west) on Deep Shore Road to the park.

DeLorme: Maryland and Delaware Atlas & Gazetteer: Page 51 D4.

Description: George Martinak deeded this land of forests, fields, and marsh to the state in 1961 for preservation as a recreational facility and natural area for the enjoyment of all. Bordered by the Choptank River and Watts Creek, this area supports a wide variety of plant and animal life.

A good boat ramp is available at the park, and shore-angling opportunities abound. Other amenities include modern campsites, hiking trails, a nature center, and a playground.

The fishing: The Upper Choptank is a typical Middle Atlantic warm-water fishery. Largemouth bass is the primary target of most anglers. However, catfish is a close second, and there are some excellent specimens in the Choptank. Crappie, perch, and bluegill fishing is also good.

Camping and lodging: Sixty-three campsites are available for trailer or tent camping, 30 of which have electric hookups. Each site is equipped with a camping pad, picnic table, and fire ring. A modern bathhouse is centrally located in each camping loop. No water hookups are available, but potable water is located around each loop. A dump station is available for trailer use.

Four camper cabins and a full-service cabin are available at the park. The full-service cabin sleeps four and overlooks the Choptank River. It comes equipped with a kitchen, bath facilities, heat, air-conditioning, and a screened-in porch and is available for rent year-round. The camper cabins sleep four and are available for rent from early spring through late fall. They are equipped with a ceiling fan, electricity, air-conditioning, an outside fire ring, grill, and picnic table. Restroom and shower facilities are located a short walk away.

For more information: Martinak State Park.

67 Lower Choptank River

Key species: Striped bass, croaker, spot, white perch, bluefish, channel and other catfish, gray trout, speckled trout, flounder, and black drum at the mouth.

Directions: From Baltimore, take the Beltway (Interstate 695) to Interstate 97 south. In Annapolis, take U.S. Highway 50 east across the Bay Bridge. Continue on US 50 south to Cambridge, where the road crosses the river.

DeLorme: Maryland and Delaware Atlas & Gazetteer: Page 42 C1, C2, and D2.

Accesses: **67a, Windy Hill Ramp.** From US 50 south near Hambleton, turn left (east) on Tarbutton Mill Road, then left (north) on Wrights Mill Road. Turn right (east) on Bruceville Road, then left (north) on Windy Hill Road and follow it to the ramp. There is limited parking here.

67b, Great Marsh Park, Cambridge. Traveling south on US 50, cross the Fred Malkus Bridge into Cambridge and turn right (west) on Maryland Street, which becomes Market Street. Turn right (north) on High Street, then left (west) on Water

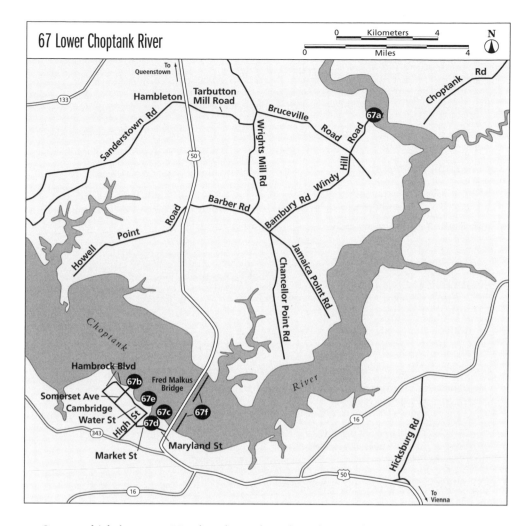

Street, which becomes Hambrock Boulevard. Make a right (north) on Somerset Avenue and follow it to the boat ramp. There is plenty of parking available, and shore fishing is also possible here.

67c, Franklin Street Ramp, Cambridge. Traveling south on US 50, cross the Fred Malkus Bridge into Cambridge and turn right (west) on Maryland Street. At Franklin Street, turn right (north) and follow it to the ramp. There is plenty of parking at this access.

67d, Cambridge Creek Ramp, Cambridge. Traveling south on US 50, cross the Fred Malkus Bridge into Cambridge and turn right (west) on Maryland Street. At Trenton Street, turn left (south) and follow it to the ramp.

67e, Long Wharf Shore Fishing Area, Cambridge. Take US 50 south across the Fred Malkus Bridge to a right (west) on Washington Street. Turn right (north) on High Street and follow it to the end by the water.

67f, Choptank River Fishing Pier. Located on the east side of US 50 on both sides of the river, next to the Fred Malkus Bridge into Cambridge, this is one of the most popular fishing piers in the area. The two sections are over a mile long. It is actually the old bridge that was left in place and maintained after the new Choptank River bridge was built. There is plenty of parking on both sides of the river.

Description: This part of the Choptank is over a mile wide and is primarily a saltwater and estuary fishery. Lots of facilities and fishing opportunities are available throughout the region.

The fishing: The first fish that show up in this area are white perch and catfish. This usually happens in February or March, but in warm winters it can be as early as January. Most anglers fish for the perch with either bloodworms or grass shrimp, but other baits like minnows and clams also work well.

Sometime in April or May, a big run of croaker comes up the river. These fish are aggressive and usually are easy to catch. Almost any bait works well. Following the croaker are the trout, both gray and speckled, and the bluefish. Peelers and soft crab are the favorites for trout, but almost any bait works well for blues.

Summer fishing in this area is on and off, depending on how warm it is. However, autumn angling is excellent, especially for striped bass.

Restrictions: Check license requirements with the Maryland Department of Natural Resources. Some areas do not require permits. Also check the possession and size limits for each species.

For more information: Dorchester County Department of Tourism; tide information, www.freetidetables.com/tides/?tti=2879.

68 Smithville Community Lake

Key species: Largemouth bass, crappie, bluegill, chain pickerel, yellow perch, brown bullhead, carp, sucker, and pumpkinseed.

Directions: From Baltimore, take the Beltway (Interstate 695) to Interstate 97 south, then take U.S. Highway 50 east across the Bay Bridge. Continue on US 50 toward Easton; near Wye Mills, make a left (east) on Maryland Highway 404. Go through Denton and, right before the Delaware border, make a right (south) on Noble Road. Look for a split-rail fence on the right; the parking lot and boat ramp are on the right (west) side of the road.

DeLorme: Maryland and Delaware Atlas & Gazetteer: Page 43 A5.

Description: Smithville is a long, narrow lake and covers 43 acres. It is shallow, with an average depth of 3 feet; the maximum is 8 feet. Many underwater branches provide hiding places for game fish.

The fishing: Smithville provides excellent fishing for bass and bluegill. The lower two-thirds of the lake has outstanding fish habitat. The many fallen trees and

Smithville Community Lake has great habitat for fish in the form of fallen trees and branches along the shore.

branches make fine places for predators and prey to hide.

Many anglers fly fish here with big bass bugs and poppers. Bream busters and mosquito patterns are also deadly.

Restrictions: There is no horsepower limitation on the lake; however, the watercraft speed limit is 6 knots. Electric trolling motors are preferred. Camping and swimming are not permitted.

For more information: Maryland Department of Natural Resources, Fisheries Service, Eastern Region Office.

69 Marshyhope Creek

Key species: Largemouth bass, crappie, bluegill and other sunfish, white perch, yellow perch, chain pickerel, shad, striped bass, channel and other catfish, and herring.

Directions: From Baltimore, take the Beltway (Interstate 695) to Interstate 97 south, then take U.S. Highway 50 east across the Bay Bridge to Easton. Take Maryland Highway 331 east, then in Preston, pick up Maryland Highway 318 east. MD 318 passes over the creek in Federalsburg.

DeLorme: Maryland and Delaware Atlas & Gazetteer: Page 43 A5 and B5.

Accesses: **69a, outflow of Smithville Community Lake.** From US 50, take Maryland Highway 404 east at Wye Mills. Past Denton, pick up Maryland Highway 313 south to Opossum Hill Road east and follow it to the bridge over the outflow.

69b, Federalsburg. From MD 318 in Federalsburg, head south on Main Street. A park with a boat ramp and seawall is on the left (east) side of the road. A walkway runs for a long distance along the banks of the Marshyhope around Federalsburg, with bank fishing possible at many points. Canoes and cartop boats can also be launched at several points.

Description: Marshyhope Creek starts at the outflow of Smithville Community Lake in Caroline County near Smithville. It is just a small stream until it reaches Federalsburg. The creek continues south, meandering past Brookview, and eventually empties into the Nanticoke River near Walnut Landing.

The fishing: Some mighty nice bass and crappie are taken in the Marshyhope. It is a great place to float trip, with terrific habitat found along the way.

Bank anglers can try their luck below the dam at the outflow of Smithville Community Lake. This is an excellent location for bluegill and crappie.

For more information: Dorchester County Department of Tourism; Maryland Department of Natural Resources, Wildlife & Heritage Service, Salisbury Office; Maryland Greenways Commission.

70 Transquaking River

Key species: Largemouth bass, crappie, rockfish, catfish, carp, pumpkinseed, yellow perch, white perch, and, in the lower reaches, croaker and spot.

Directions: From Baltimore, take the Beltway (Interstate 695) to Interstate 97 south, then take U.S. Highway 50 east across the Bay Bridge. Continue on US 50 past Cambridge. The road passes over the river above Higgins Pond near Hicksburg.

DeLorme: Maryland and Delaware Atlas & Gazetteer: Page 42 D3.

Accesses: **70a, Airey Ramp.** From Cambridge, take US 50 east to Percy May Road southwest to Drawbridge Road west. Watch for the ramp on the south side of the road by the bridge.

70b, Bestpitch Ramp. From Cambridge, take US 50 east to Bucktown Road south to Bestpitch Ferry Road southeast. The ramp is on the southeast side of the bridge.

Description: The Transquaking River is over 23 miles long and located in Dorchester County. Its headwaters are near the east New Market area; it runs through the Fishing Bay Wildlife Management Area and finally empties into Chesapeake Bay about 7 miles south of Bestpitch.

The fishing: The Transquaking River and its tributaries support good fish populations. Anglers have a chance to catch such saltwater and freshwater species as largemouth bass, rockfish, white and yellow perch, black crappie, catfish, carp, and pumpkinseed.

For more information: Blackwater National Wildlife Refuge; Dorchester County Department of Tourism; Maryland Department of Natural Resources, Wildlife & Heritage Service, Salisbury Office; Maryland Greenways Commission; boat ramp information, Dorchester County Road Department, (410) 228-2920.

71 Blackwater River and Little Blackwater River

Key species: Largemouth bass, striped bass, chain pickerel, crappie, channel and other catfish, yellow perch, white perch, and bluegill and other sunfish.

Directions: From Baltimore, take the Beltway (Interstate 695) to Interstate 97 south, then take U.S. Highway 50 east across the Bay Bridge. Continue on US 50 to Cambridge.

DeLorme: Maryland and Delaware Atlas & Gazetteer: Page 32 B2.

Accesses: **71a, bridge over Little Blackwater River.** In Cambridge, pick up Washington Street (Maryland Highway 343) west to a left (south) on Race Street, which becomes Maple Dam Road. In Seward, turn right (west) on Key Wallace Drive and follow it to the bridge over the Little Blackwater River. Fishing is possible along the road shoulders but is not legal from the bridge. Canoes and kayaks can be launched from the bank.

71b, Shorters Wharf Ramp. In Cambridge, pick up Washington Street (MD 343) west to Race Street south, which becomes Maple Dam Road. Continue on Maple Dam Road to the ramp on the right (west) side of the road.

71c, Maryland Highway 335 Bridge. In Cambridge, pick up Washington Street (MD 343) west to Race Street south. In Seward, turn right (west) on Key Wallace Drive, then turn left (south) on Maryland Highway 335 and follow it to the bridge. Fishing is possible along the road shoulders but is not legal from the bridge. Canoes and kayaks can be launched from the bank.

Description: The Blackwater and the Little Blackwater are two Eastern Shore meandering rivers that pass through fresh and brackish marshes before emptying into Fishing Bay. It is a pleasant area, with great bird- and other wildlife-watching opportunities.

The fishing: The most popular fishing areas are located near the bridges over the Little Blackwater River on Key Wallace Drive and the Blackwater River on MD 335. Though fishing can be described as fair to poor at both of the above locations, at other times, especially in the spring, white perch angling can be fast and furious. Carp fishing with corn at that time is also excellent.

Restrictions: Only canoes and kayaks may be launched in the Blackwater National Wildlife Refuge. No fishing from the banks is allowed in the refuge. Check with the Maryland Department of Natural Resources for up-to-date regulations.

For more information: Blackwater National Wildlife Refuge; Maryland Department of Natural Resources, Fisheries Service, Eastern Region Office.

72 Deal Island Boat Harbor

Key species: Speckled trout, gray trout, striped bass, croaker, flounder, red drum, black drum, white perch, bluefish, blue crab, and spot.

Directions: From Baltimore, take the Beltway (Interstate 695) to Interstate 97 south, then take U.S. Highway 50 east across the Bay Bridge. Continue on US 50 past Cambridge, then take the Salisbury Bypass to U.S. Highway 13 south. In Princess Anne, make a right (west) on Deal Island Road (Maryland Highway 363) and fol-

Holland Island is accessible from the boat launch at Deal Island.

low it through Dames Quarter and Chance and over the bridge. The harbor is on the right (north) side of the road.

DeLorme: Maryland and Delaware Atlas & Gazetteer: Page 25 A4.

Description: The boat harbor at Deal Island can be a busy place during the height of the season, but for the most part, it is rather quiet. Plenty of parking is available.

The fishing: Fishing is possible off the docks and the beach beside the bridge over the Upper Thoroughfare. Most saltwater species are caught here, including speckled and gray trout, rockfish, croaker, and spot. A good boat ramp gives access to Tangier Sound, Hoopers Strait, and Holland and Bloodsworth Islands, and it is about a 6-mile run to the target ship off Smith Island.

For more information: Maryland Department of Natural Resources, Fisheries Service, Eastern Region Office.

73 Impoundment and Creeks at the End of Riley Roberts Road

Key species: Blue crab, white perch, speckled trout, gray trout, red drum, black drum, rockfish, spot, croaker, and flounder.

Directions: From Baltimore, take the Beltway (Interstate 695) to Interstate 97 south, then take U.S. Highway 50 east across the Bay Bridge. Travel past Cambridge and take the Salisbury Bypass to U.S. Highway 13 south. In Princess Anne, make a right (west) on Deal Island Road (Maryland Highway 363) and follow it to Dames Quarter. Make a left (south) on Riley Roberts Road and take it to the end. The road can be rough at times but is almost always passable.

DeLorme: Maryland and Delaware Atlas & Gazetteer: Page 25 A4.

Description: This is a really pretty area, with marsh almost as far as one can see. It is alive with bird, mammal, and marine species, providing lots of opportunity to observe wildlife.

The fishing: The state impounded this large area to aid waterfowl, and it also grows some very large, fat crabs. Good fishing for white perch, spot, croaker, and some striped bass may be had in the creeks. Fair ramps give access to the impoundment, the creeks, and the Manokin River. This is a good speckled trout area, and occasionally some large red drum pass though.

For more information: Maryland Department of Natural Resources, Fisheries Service, Eastern Region Office.

74 Monie Bay

Key species: Blue crab, white perch, speckled trout, gray trout, red drum, black drum, rockfish, spot, croaker, and flounder.

Directions: From Baltimore, take the Beltway (Interstate 695) to Interstate 97 south, then take U.S. Highway 50 east across the Bay Bridge. Travel past Cambridge and take the Salisbury Bypass to U.S. Highway 13 south. In Princess Anne, make a right (west) on Deal Island Road (Maryland Highway 363) and follow it to Dames Quarter. Just as you are entering Dames Quarter from the east on MD 363, make a right (north) on Messick Road and follow it to the end.

DeLorme: Maryland and Delaware Atlas & Gazetteer: Page 33 D4.

Description: This location is at the end of a dead-end road. It is a quiet area, and plenty of parking is available.

The fishing: This is an excellent place to launch a small boat to troll for rockfish along Monie Bay's marsh bank. In addition, white perch and spot fishing can be great in this bay. Many perch and an occasional linesider are also caught by casting off the dock.

For more information: Maryland Department of Natural Resources, Fisheries Service, Eastern Region Office.

75 Wicomico Creek

Key species: White perch, largemouth bass, and catfish.

Directions: From Baltimore, take the Beltway (Interstate 695) to Interstate 97 south, then take U.S. Highway 50 east across the Bay Bridge. Continue on US 50 to Salisbury, but do not take the Salisbury Bypass. Take Business US 50 instead and go .south on Business U.S. Highway 13. In Fruitland, turn right (west) on South Division Street, then left (south) on Allen Cutoff Road. Make another left (west) on Allen Road and follow it through Allen to a small park on the west side of the road. The access to Wicomico Creek is on the right.

DeLorme: Maryland and Delaware Atlas & Gazetteer: Page 33 C6.

Description: This site is located in a town park. The town itself has become quite developed in recent years, but good fishing can still be had. It is possible to launch a cartop boat or canoe from the bank.

The fishing: Wicomico Creek is an excellent early-season (February to May) white perch fishery. Nice catfish can be caught here, and largemouth bass are also available for the persistent.

For more information: Maryland Department of Natural Resources, Fisheries Service, Eastern Region Office.

Wicomico River and Tributaries

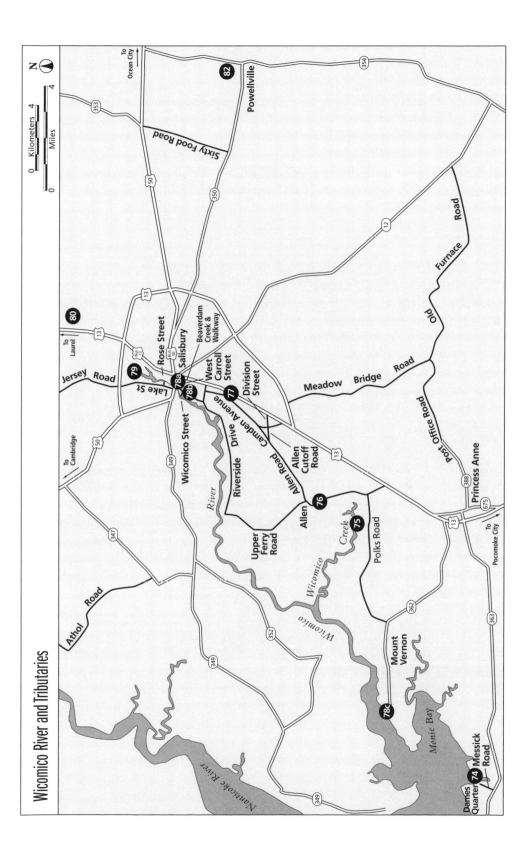

Calico in the Spring

Eastern Shore freshwater anglers are often shocked to find that one of their favorite quarries, crappie, is or has been considered trash fish in many parts of the country.

A good example is northern Vermont, where this species is known as strawberry or calico bass. In the recent past, when these fish were unlucky enough to be caught, anglers would break their necks and throw them up into the grass. Fortunately, this has changed in recent years due to the influx of transplants from other areas of the country. There is also now a commercial fishery in Lake Champlain for crappie to be sold in Montreal, Canada.

Many Delmarva anglers really enjoy fishing for and eating crappie. While this species can be found throughout the upper Wicomico River around Salisbury, there are a few locations worth mentioning. One of the best is where the Wicomico River flows under Isabella Street. Foot access is problematic here, as the area has been fenced and posted, and it is also a little difficult to park nearby. The upper river can, however, be approached with a small boat or canoe.

Another good area is in the East Branch below the falls and rapids flowing out of the park on the corner of East Main Street and Snow Hill Road. The dock adjacent to the boat ramp off Riverside Drive is also a very convenient location, as is the entire walkway along the East Branch below the Salisbury Times Building. The park on the corner of West Main and Lake has convenient parking as well as benches and a nice rail to fish from. If it's windy and cold, you can sit in your vehicle and drink coffee while you watch your rods for action.

Allen Pond is one our favorite locations for spring crappie. The shoreline of this lake is quite accessible for the shore-bound angler. You do, however, have to make a rather long cast to get out to the crappie holding area; therefore, a weighted float is a great asset.

Rigs are quite simple for these guys. A #4 to #6 sproat-style hook, Carlisle, or beak hook tied a few feet below a bobber is the ticket. A small split shot 6 inches above the hook will help get the bait down to where the fish are schooling.

When crappie are ready to feed, they can be aggressive, but it sometimes takes a little bit of technique to entice them into action. Jerking the line in a manner that makes it appear as though the minnow is trying to escape could be advantageous.

The favorite bait of many Delmarva calico anglers is a live, small mud minnow (available at most tackle and bait shops); however, small bucktails and plastic jigs also work well. For flavor, many anglers will put a minnow or piece of squid on the tip of the jig.

Crappie are not only real pretty, but also great table fare. Many are large enough to provide two good fillets. When caught in the early season, there are not very many other piscatorial treats that are tastier.

Spring crappie fishing is great family fun. We have described only a small number of good locations—Delmarva anglers have lots of access to some very productive areas. Try a few of the popular places, then go looking for your own secret honey hole.

76 Allen Pond

Key species: Crappie and largemouth bass.

Directions: From Baltimore, take the Beltway (Interstate 695) to Interstate 97 south, then take U.S. Highway 50 east across the Bay Bridge. Continue on US 50 to Salisbury, but do not take the Salisbury Bypass. Take Business US 50 instead and go south on Business U.S. Highway 13. In Fruitland, turn right (west) on South Division Street, then left (south) on Allen Cutoff Road. Make another left on Allen Road and follow it to a small park on the west side of the road. The access to Allen Pond is on the left (east) side of the road.

DeLorme: Maryland and Delaware Atlas & Gazetteer: Page 33 C6.

Description: Allen Pond is a small impoundment. A lot of development has occurred in the area in the past few years, but some good angling opportunities still exist. A cartop boat or canoe can be launched from the bank.

The fishing: Crappie fishing is excellent in this pond, especially during warm spells in the winter. Try it as a low-pressure front is passing through. A weighted float is helpful here, because long casts may be required when casting from the bank.

For more information: Maryland Department of Natural Resources, Fisheries Service, Eastern Region Office.

77 Tony Tank Creek

Key species: Bluegill, crappie, largemouth bass, white perch, yellow perch, and catfish.

Directions: From Baltimore, take the Beltway (Interstate 695) to Interstate 97 south, then take U.S. Highway 50 east across the Bay Bridge. Continue on US 50 to Salisbury, but do not take the Salisbury Bypass. Take Business US 50 instead and go south on Business U.S. Highway 13. Follow Business US 13 to the bridge right before the Wal-Mart on the left (east) side of the road. Parking here is limited.

DeLorme: Maryland and Delaware Atlas & Gazetteer: Page 34 C1.

Description: Another excellent Salisbury location is the bridge over Tony Tank, a dammed-up area of Tony Tank Creek. The bridge has a sidewalk, and it is also possible to fish the banks alongside the structure.

The fishing: There are numerous bluegill here, some quite large, making it a great place to take a kid fishing.

For more information: Maryland Department of Natural Resources, Fisheries Service, Eastern Region Office.

78 Wicomico River

Key species: Largemouth bass, bluegill and other sunfish, crappie, white perch, yellow perch, channel and other catfish, a few shad species, herring, American eel, and striped bass. Many saltwater species near the mouth, including croaker, speckled trout, gray trout, flounder, spot, black drum, red drum, and bluefish.

Directions: From Baltimore, take the Beltway (Interstate 695) to Interstate 97 south, then take U.S. Highway 50 east across the Bay Bridge. Continue on US 50 to Salisbury, but do not take the Salisbury Bypass. Take Business US 50 instead, which crosses one of the branches of the Wicomico right in town.

DeLorme: Maryland and Delaware Atlas & Gazetteer: Page 33 D4; Page 34 B1.

Accesses: **78a, walkway along Beaverdam Creek.** From Business US 50 in Salisbury, take Business U.S. Highway 13 south and turn right (west) on West Carroll Street. This street follows Beaverdam Creek, which empties into the Wicomico River, and the walkway runs between the road and the creek. This is a great area for bank fishing.

78b, pier and boat ramp off Riverside Drive. From Business US 50 in Salisbury, take Business US 13 south and turn right (west) on West Carroll Street. Make a left on Riverside Drive (south), then a right on Wicomico Street. The pier is located on the right (north) alongside the boat ramp behind the quick-stop store. This area is in a small park on the banks of the Wicomico River. The pier is quite modern, and picnic benches are available.

78c, ramp at Mount Vernon. From Salisbury, take US 13 south to Princess Anne, then turn right (west) on Mount Vernon Road (Maryland Highway 362). In Mount Vernon, turn right (north) on Dorsey Avenue and follow it to the end. There are a couple of piers here and a paved parking lot with room for a number of trailers. Some bank fishing is also available.

Description: The Wicomico River is formed by the outflow of a few ponds around Salisbury. From here it meanders about 10 miles through Fruitland, past Whitehaven and Mount Vernon, then empties into Tangier Sound.

The fishing: Like many Eastern Shore streams, the fishing in this river is excellent and very diverse. Freshwater and anadromous fish abound upstream, while near the mouth, salty and anadromous species are predominant.

Upstream, around Salisbury, the most common fish are the various sunfish species. Most anglers use bait like night crawlers or grubs; however, small jigs are an excellent choice. Use jigs with hooks no larger than #8, but #10s or #12s are even better. Fly fishers could also have a ball with these small scrappers. Both dry and wet flies will work, and anything that looks like a small insect or larvae would be a good choice.

Crappie are also abundant, with some that run up to 2½ pounds. Live small minnows are best, but small grubby tails and jig/minnow combos are also excellent.

Fish around both the old and newer dock. These fish are very structure-specific. Minnow-imitating wet flies and streamers are killers for calicos.

Bucketmouths are also abundant in the tidal river. Fish around structures with large swimming plugs, plastics, and surface lures. Bass bugs and poppers work well for fly fishers.

White perch make a run up the Wicomico River from Tangier Sound in the spring. They are one of the tastiest fish caught in these parts. The favorite bait for whities—or as they are known locally, black perch—is pieces of bloodworms. However, night crawlers, small minnows, and small chunks of clam and squid are also effective. Though overlooked by most anglers, small lead-head bucktail jigs are also excellent.

Various species of catfish are available almost year-round. Most anglers fish with night crawlers or commercially bought stinkbaits. Fish the bottom with a 2/0 to 5/0 hook.

Shad species run up the Wicomico in the spring. Darts and other small jigs are the favorites of many anglers, and white hair with a red head is preferred. Note: Check the regulations carefully before fishing for this species. Most shad species have been closed to all angling.

Along with the shad, herring invade the river from Tangier Sound each spring. Fish for them with flies or a plain gold hook. These fish are great pickled, and be sure to save some for bait.

The upstream area of the Wicomico is a year-round fishery. Even during the coldest winters, crappie and sunfish can be caught.

Downstream and near the mouth, the fishing starts with white perch, usually sometime in February. When the water warms, other species begin to show up. Striped bass make an appearance, as do channel catfish. In May, croaker make a run up Tangier Sound to the mouths of most of the rivers. These fish are followed by speckled and gray trout, red and black drum, spot, flounder, and the other salty species.

Restrictions: Carefully check the shad regulations with the Maryland Department of Natural Resources. Largemouth bass, striped bass, and other fish are also regulated.

For more information: Maryland Department of Natural Resources, Fisheries Service, Eastern Region Office.

79 Johnson's Pond

Key species: Largemouth bass, chain pickerel, black crappie, yellow perch, bluegill and other sunfish, and carp.

Directions: From Baltimore, take the Beltway (Interstate 695) to Interstate 97 south, then take U.S. Highway 50 east across the Bay Bridge. Continue on US 50 to Salisbury, but do not take the Salisbury Bypass. Take Business US 50 instead and go north on Business U.S. Highway 13. Turn left (west) on Isabella Street, then make a right (north) on Lake Street. Turn right (east) on Rose Street to the gravel parking lot with a paved boat ramp.

DeLorme: Maryland and Delaware Atlas & Gazetteer: Page 34 B1.

Description: This 104-acre pond is the largest fishing impoundment on the Eastern Shore. Its maximum depth is 11 feet. The pond has two principal tributaries, which form north and east forks. The east fork is relatively shallow with lots of rooted aquatic vegetation and a small amount of submerged timber. The north fork is deeper and contains many standing trees, stumps, docks, and rooted aquatic vegetation.

The main pool area has been decorated with numerous evergreen tree fish "attractors." The banks are steep along the eastern shore of the main pool, and there are many trees in the water; however, most of the habitat in the lower third of the pond exists on the western shore. This habitat consists of trees, brush, and limbs. Numerous private docks located throughout the pond provide excellent fish habitat.

The fishing: Johnson's Pond is a Special Bass Management Area. Anglers can find information pertaining to these special regulations in the *Maryland Freshwater Sportfishing Guide* and also on signs posted at the launching ramp. The regulations help maintain a well-balanced bass/bluegill fishery, and excellent fishing for both these species exists here.

Anglers may also occasionally catch other species, including black crappie, pumpkinseed, yellow and white perch, chain pickerel, brown bullhead, and common carp. While not typically targeted by anglers, gizzard shad, golden shiner, and chubsucker are also present in the pond and provide an important forage source for the predatory fishes.

Restrictions: Camping and swimming are prohibited.

For more information: Maryland Department of Natural Resources, Fisheries Service, Eastern Region Office.

80 Leonard's Mill Pond

Key species: Largemouth bass, chain pickerel, bluegill and other sunfish, and channel catfish.

Directions: From Baltimore, take the Beltway (Interstate 695) to Interstate 97 south, then take U.S. Highway 50 east across the Bay Bridge to the Salisbury Bypass. Go north on U.S. Highway 13 and take the first left (west) after crossing over the bridge to the lake. This is the parkig lot of an information center.

DeLorme: Maryland and Delaware Atlas & Gazetteer: Page 34 A1.

Description: Leonard's Mill Pond is about 30 acres in size and has a maximum depth of 8 feet. The pond is surrounded by private residences, which have piers and bulkheads to fish around. There is some downed timber, and both forks have many stumps, with the south fork being deeper than the north fork.

The fishing: Leonard's Mill Pond is a Trophy Bass Management Area, and the regulations are posted on signs at the launching ramp. The special regulations help maintain a well-balanced bass/bluegill fishery. Excellent fishing for both of these species exists here. Anglers may also occasionally catch other species, including pumpkinseed, yellow bullhead, golden shiner, creek chubsucker, black crappie, chain pickerel, and common carp.

Restrictions: Camping and swimming are prohibited.

For more information: Maryland Department of Natural Resources, Fisheries Service, Eastern Region Office.

81 Nanticoke River, Maryland

Key species: Largemouth bass, striped bass, chain pickerel, crappie, channel and other catfish, bluegill and other sunfish, white perch, and yellow perch.

The Nanticoke River in Maryland is an excellent warm-water fishery.

Directions: From Baltimore, take the Beltway (Interstate 695) to Interstate 97 south, then take U.S. Highway 50 east across the Bay Bridge through Cambridge. US 50 passes over the Nanticoke River at Vienna.

DeLorme: Maryland and Delaware Atlas & Gazetteer: Page 33 A5, B4, and C4; Page 43 D5.

Accesses: **81a, Sharptown Ramp and bank fishing.** Continue on US 50 east from Vienna. At Mardella Springs, turn left (north) on Maryland Highway 313 to Sharp town and follow the signs to Cherry Beach.

81b, Vienna Boat Ramp and Seawall. In Vienna, take Maryland Highway 331 south to Race Street and turn left (east). Race Street ends at the ramp.

81c, Tyaskin Boat Ramp. Continue on US 50 east from Vienna. Near Hebron, turn right (south) on Maryland Highway 347, continue through Quantico, and turn right (west) on Maryland Highway 349. At Wetipqin Road, go right (north) and follow it to the ramp on the creek right before Tyaskin.

81d, Nanticoke Harbor Boat Ramp. Continue on US 50 east from Vienna. Near Hebron, turn right (south) on MD 347, continue through Quantico, and turn right (west) on MD 349. Continue through Bivalve and Jesterville to Nanticoke, where the ramp is on the right (west) side of the road.

Description: The Nanticoke River enters Maryland from Delaware near Sharptown. It is a typical lowland Chesapeake Bay tributary. Along its course, much of the river's shoreline is marshland and therefore prime breeding ground for many species.

The fishing: This stream is a terrific warm-water fishery for most of its course. Largemouth bass do very well here. The river has an excellent run of white perch in the spring. In fact, it is one the earliest waters where these fish can be caught on the entire Eastern Shore. One of the areas where anglers fish for these early perch is around Tyaskin and Roaring Point.

Nice channel cats are relatively easy to catch. Casting off the bulkhead in Vienna is an excellent place to try. White perch are also caught here.

Speckled and gray trout can be caught from May through October near the mouth of the river. A few black and red drum may also be taken in this area.

For more information: Maryland Department of Natural Resources, Fisheries Service, Eastern Region Office.

82 Adkins Mill Pond

Key species: Largemouth bass, chain pickerel, yellow perch, white perch, and bluegill.

Directions: From Baltimore, take the Beltway (Interstate 695) to Interstate 97 south, then take U.S. Highway 50 east across the Bay Bridge, through Cambridge, toward

Salisbury. Do not take the Salisbury Bypass; instead, continue on Business US 50 through the city. Make a right (east) on Maryland Highway 350 (Mount Hermon Road) toward Powellville, then turn left (north) on Maryland Highway 354 (Willards-Whiton Road). The pond is on your left, toward the west.

DeLorme: Maryland and Delaware Atlas & Gazetteer: Page 34 C3.

Description: Adkins Mill Pond is a 4-acre impoundment in south-central Wicomico County. The pond is tannic and shallow, with the deepest area near its upper reaches. These upper reaches are heavily forested, with some bald cypress. Four walking trails exist for accessing this area. A picnic pavilion, modern restrooms, and a dock are available for public use.

The fishing: Adkins Mill Pond supports a standard bass/bluegill fishery and is managed accordingly. Anglers may also occasionally catch other species, including pumpkinseed, brown bullhead, golden shiner, creek chubsucker, black crappie, chain pickerel, common carp, blue-spotted sunfish, and American eel.

For more information: Maryland Department of Natural Resources, Wildlife & Heritage Service, Salisbury Office.

83 Assateague Island

Key species: Striped bass, bluefish, kingfish (whiting), croaker, spot, flounder, red drum, black drum, gray trout, and speckled trout.

Directions: From Baltimore, take the Beltway (Interstate 695) to Interstate 97 south, then take U.S. Highway 50 east across the Bay Bridge, through Cambridge and Salisbury, toward Ocean City. Before the bridge to Ocean City, turn right (south) on Maryland Highway 611 (Stephen Decatur Highway). Follow this road to Assateague State Park and then to the beach. Parking is available, but four-wheel-drive vehicles may drive on the beach; see restrictions below.

DeLorme: Maryland and Delaware Atlas & Gazetteer: Page 35 C6.

Description: The beach runs for many miles, north to Ocean City Inlet and south to Virginia.

The fishing: This is the premier surf-casting location in Maryland. Depending on the season, anglers may catch striped bass, bluefish, spot, skate, whiting (kingfish), flounder, and many other species.

Restrictions: A permit is required to drive on the beach. Contact Assateague State Park for information.

Camping: More than 300 sites are available at Assateague State Park, some with hookups.

For more information: Assateague State Park.

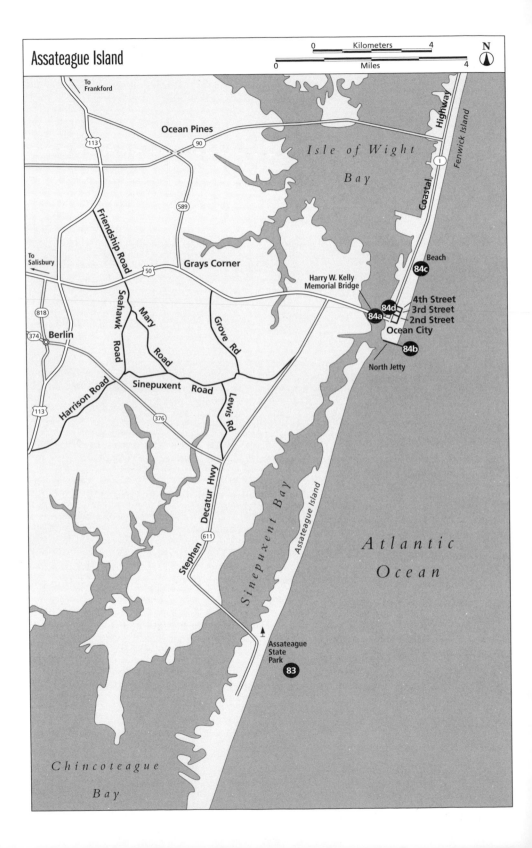

Assateague Island

84 Ocean City Area

Key species: Flounder, striped bass, tautog, tuna species, marlin species, sea bass, croaker, spot, bluefish, black drum, red drum, sea trout, and whiting.

Directions: From Baltimore, take the Beltway (Interstate 695) to Interstate 97 south, then take U.S. Highway 50 east across the Bay Bridge, through Cambridge and Salisbury, all the way to its end.

DeLorme: Maryland and Delaware Atlas & Gazetteer: Page 35 B6 and C6.

Accesses: **84a, US 50 Bridge.** This bridge is at the end of US 50. You can either park before it or in the streets of Ocean City. Many fish this structure at night for striped bass, weakfish, and bluefish. Some anglers use lures like plastic-tail lead-heads and troll by walking or cast around the pilings. Day anglers often take flounder and, in the few rocky areas, tautog.

84b, North Jetty. After crossing the US 50 Bridge, turn right (south) and follow the road to its end. A big parking lot is available right next to the jetty. This jetty is relatively flat and fairly easy to negotiate; however, anglers should wear slip-proof shoes and/or boots. All the species mentioned for the Ocean City area can be taken off the jetty. Tautog are popular in the spring and fall.

84c, Ocean City beach. The beach runs the entire distance of Ocean City for many miles. Parking can be a problem in some areas, but leaving your vehicle on a side street is possible. The beach is constantly changing, so good fishing locations are difficult to describe. Learn to read the beach to be a successful surf caster. Many species can be caught, but the most popular are striped bass, bluefish, whiting (kingfish), skate, and spot.

84d, bulkhead between Second and Fourth Streets. After crossing the US 50 Bridge, head north. Turn west (left) on Second, Third, or Fourth Streets and head toward the end. The bulkhead runs for a number of blocks in both directions. This is a comfortable place for shore-bound anglers who are not into surf casting. Depending on the time of year, flounder, striped bass, weakfish, croaker, spot, and many other species are available. This is an excellent tautog fishing area because when the bulkhead was built, many giant boulders were used to hold it in place. Be prepared to lose a bunch of rigs in the rocks.

Description: Ocean City is a resort town on the Atlantic. All amenities are available.

The fishing: This city is a premier destination for ocean fishing in Maryland. Whether you are interested in leisurely fishing from the shore along the bulkhead, climbing the rocks of the jetties to try your luck at some 'tog or striped bass, casting into the suds for slammer blues, drifting the inlet for nice flounder, or finding an offshore big-game adventure, Ocean City has it all.

Shore-bound and small-boat anglers head to the coast for a number of species. One of the favorites is the shell cruncher, tautog. These fish are extremely tough and

Luxury Head Boat Fishing

The gentle roll as we passed through Ocean City inlet was soothing, and it stimulated images of big tautog pumping on the business end of my outfit. Most folks might think I'm crazy, but after a lifetime of fishing on head boats, the above phenomenon, when mixed with a hint of diesel exhaust, further stimulates that optimistic angler area of my brain.

Within 30 minutes the boat was double anchored over a nice piece of jagged bottom. My sinker hit the bottom, but before I could retrieve the slack in my line, the big 'tog was banging on the green crab bait. After a few tastes, he decided it was exactly what he ordered for dinner. With a powerful lunge, he grabbed the crab and, with a lightning-speed dash, headed back into his lair.

My heavyweight rod and Daiwa M-S300 Millionaire reel loaded with 40-pound-test Maxima line, in conjunction with my muscle, stopped the run. He reluctantly gave ground—or should I say, water—and came out of the wreck angry that he was being pulled from his home in a direction he didn't want to go. His fury was expressed by the pumping of my rod that was whacking the railing like an elementary school kid practicing drumming. I'm a big guy, but I was barely able to hold my rod high enough so the fish would work against the pole and not the line. He ran around the stern, and my mind imagined a bird's nest. But no one was fishing there, because I was on Captain Monty Hawkins's *Morning Star* out of Ocean City, Maryland.

Captain Monty runs a very interesting and unique operation that specializes in precision fishing of the natural, shipwreck, and artificial reefs off the coasts of Maryland and Virginia. Instead of crowding folks in, he charges a bit more and limits the number of anglers to 25. The *Morning Star* is an ultramodern, very comfortable 55-foot party boat. The day I went on her, she had just been slipped back into the water after winter maintenance and was sparkling bright.

Monty belongs to a growing movement among head boat captains; that is, he has one of the strongest conservation ethics I have ever encountered in this group of folks. In fact, even before the feds and the state began regulating many fisheries, Monty had set size and per-passenger bag limits on some species, including tautog and sea bass. He says he remembers the days during the 1980s when the angling in this part of the world hit the pits, and he doesn't want that to happen again.

Monty is a great head boat captain but would have been an even better scientist if that's what he wanted to do with his life. I've met very few in his business with as great a need to know how oceanic systems work. To this end he tags hundreds if not thousands of fish every year in an effort to discover how they move around. In the long run, this information will be invaluable in management of the fishery.

In addition, Captain Monty is very active in the movement to create and protect habitat for fish. On the day I was out with him, we fished on a number of artificial reefs that were placed offshore by the Ocean City Reef Association.

Unless the winter is extremely cold, there is year-round fishing out of Ocean City, but there aren't many boats that run. The *Morning Star* will venture out almost anytime the weather is acceptable, starting the year fishing for big tautog. As the weather warms, the first sea bass begin to show up in the catch. In late spring they begin to dominate, and by midsummer the take is pretty much 100 percent sea bass.

At times, other species are mixed in. For example, during the summer and fall, bruiser bluefish will often cruise higher up in the water column. On these occasions, some customers will tie on diamond jigs, tin squids, or other lures and take advantage of the opportunity to get a few choppers for the grill. Triggerfish, croaker, and sea trout are among the other species that may be caught.

If you wish to use your own tackle, bring a stout rod with 40-pound test for 'tog or a medium outfit with 30-pound line for sea bass. Most anglers use either razor-sharp hooks like the Mustad Ultra-Point in sizes 1/0 to 5/0, or if you are a traditionalist like myself, Mustad Virginia-style hooks in sizes 2 to 6. If the wreck is not too sticky, a double-hook rig can be employed, but where snags are abundant, use only a single hook.

For 'tog, the favorite bait is green crabs, but clams and other crustaceans also work. Personally, I prefer to pop off the top shell of the crab, then cut it in half and trim most of the legs off. Others use whole crab with the top shell crushed, and some folks put both hooks into the same piece of bait.

The large 'tog that ran around the stern that day continued to fight for a few minutes before coming to the surface. He was a large male with a big light-colored dot on his side. The fish probably weighed about 8 or 9 pounds, and he was just too beautiful to kill. So the mate netted him, and after a few photos (or should I say, since we are in the twenty-first century, digital images), he was tagged and released to fight another day.

If you are tired of crowded head boats and want to fish with a very knowledgeable and conservation-minded captain, give Captain Monty a buzz at (410) 520-2076 or visit his Web site, www.morningstarfishing.com. You will see what a difference 100 percent effort and lots of room at the rail can make in your fishing day!

The Ocean City area has great opportunities for 'tog fishing.

use some very substantial teeth to crush crabs and other hard-shelled creatures. As a result, anglers either use cut-up green or blue crab as bait.

For more information: Roland E. Powell Convention Center. For a comprehensive fishing report and charter boat information, check www.atbeach.com/fishing. For a short daily fishing report, see www.ocfishing.com/report.html.

85 Pocomoke River

Key species: In the lower river, blue crab, white perch, speckled trout, gray trout, red drum, black drum, rockfish, spot, croaker, and flounder. In the upper river, largemouth bass, bluegill and other sunfish, crappie, white perch, yellow perch, channel and other catfish, a few shad species, herring, American eel, and striped bass.

Directions: From Baltimore, take the Beltway (Interstate 695) to Interstate 97 south, then take U.S. Highway 50 east across the Bay Bridge. Continue on US 50 past Cambridge and take the Salisbury Bypass to U.S. Highway 13 south. US 13 crosses the river at Pocomoke City.

DeLorme: Maryland and Delaware Atlas & Gazetteer: Page 26 B2, B1, and C1; Page 27 A4.

Accesses: **85a, Cedar Hall Ramp.** From US 13 south in Pocomoke City, take the Pocomoke Beltway west to Cedar Hall Road (Maryland Highway 371) west. After passing through Cedar Hall, pick up Cedar Hall Wharf Road and follow it to the ramp.

85b, Rehobeth Ramp and Seawall. From US 13 a few miles before Pocomoke City, turn right (west) on Rehobeth Road (Maryland Highway 667) and follow it to Coventry Parish Road. Turn left (south) and follow Coventry Parish Road to the end, keeping to the left at a fork. A nice seawall is located at the boat ramp. Excellent white perch fishing can be had here, especially in the spring. Some years, croaker and spot also come this far up the river. A few striped bass are caught, too.

85c, Pocomoke City Seawall. Before the river crossing in Pocomoke City on US 13 south, turn right (east) on Market Street. Follow Market Street across the bridge; the seawall will be obvious.

85d, Winter Haven Ramp and Pier. Heading north on US 13 in Pocomoke, turn right (north) on Winter Quarter Road before the Pocomoke River Bridge and follow the road to the water.

85e, ramp and pier at Shad Landing at Pocomoke River State Park. From US 13 south in Pocomoke City, turn left (east) on U.S. Highway 113. The park is located on the left a few miles before Snow Hill. Once in the park, follow the signs to the boat ramp.

85f, Byrd Park (Snow Hill) Ramp, Pier, and Seawall. From US 13 south in Pocomoke City, turn left (east) on US 113. Make a left (north) on Market Street

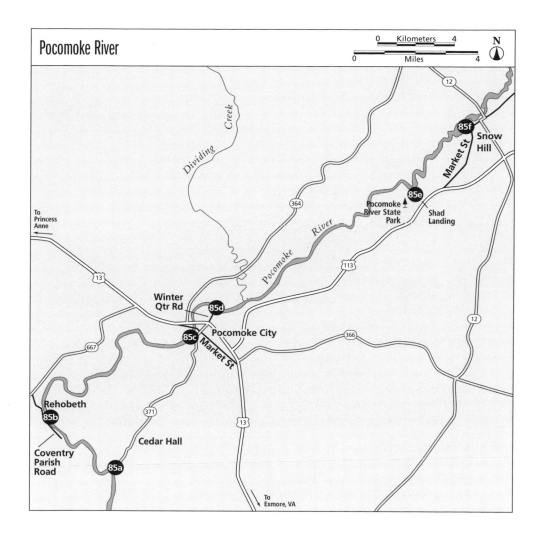

(Maryland Highway 394) and turn left (west) into Byrd Park on Ball Park Road. The dock, ramp, and pier are straight ahead.

Description: The headwaters of the Pocomoke River are found in southern Delaware. The river is fed by a number of creeks and flows southwest toward Snow Hill, Maryland, where it tumbles over a falls and becomes freshwater tidal. The river widens and eventually meanders past Pocomoke City, entering Pocomoke Sound downstream of Shelltown.

The fishing: Like most larger Eastern Shore streams, the fishing in this river is excellent and very diverse. Freshwater and anadromous fish abound upstream, while near the mouth, salty and anadromous species are predominant.

Upstream between Pocomoke City and Snow Hill is the freshwater tidal area of the river. The most common species is white perch, with yellow perch and crappie close seconds. Sunfish species are also plentiful. Most anglers will use bait such

The Winter Haven ramp and pier provides good access to the Pocomoke River.

as night crawlers or grubs for the perch and sunfish and small minnows for the crappie; however, small jigs are also excellent. Use ones with hooks no larger than #8, but #10s or #12s are even better. Fly fishers can also have fun with these small scrappers. Both dry and wet flies will work, and anything that looks like a small insect or larvae would be a good choice.

Good-size bucketmouths are abundant in the tidal river. Finding structures of fallen trees is important. Large swimming plugs, plastics, and surface lures are excellent choices, and bass bugs and poppers work well for fly fishers.

Very large yellow perch start hitting in this area in February; strict regulations apply. Various species of catfish are available almost year-round. Most folks fish with night crawlers or commercially bought stinkbaits. Fish the bottom with a 2/0 to 5/0 hook.

Shad and herring species run up the Pocomoke in the spring. Darts and other small jigs are the favorites of most anglers, and white hair with a red head is preferred. Note: Check the regulations carefully before fishing for this species. White shad have been closed to all angling, and other shad may follow suit.

Downstream and near the mouth, white perch start hitting around Shelltown and Rehobeth in February and March. When the water warms, other species begin to show up. Striped bass make an appearance near the mouth in the spring. In May, the mouth of the river and the sound are among the earliest areas in Maryland where croaker are taken. These fish are followed by both gray and speckled trout, red and black drum, spot, flounder, and the other salty species.

For more information: Maryland Department of Natural Resources, Fisheries Service, Eastern Region Office.

86 Janes Island State Park

Key species: Gray trout, speckled trout, striped bass, white perch, spot, croaker, red drum, black drum, blue crab, and flounder.

Directions: From Baltimore, take the Beltway (Interstate 695) to Interstate 97 south, then take U.S. Highway 50 east across the Bay Bridge. Continue on US 50 past Cambridge and take the Salisbury Bypass to U.S. Highway 13 south. Turn right (west) on Maryland Highway 413 and follow it toward Crisfield. Take a right (north) on Plantation Avenue, then turn left (west) on Jacksonville Road and follow it to the park entrance.

DeLorme: Maryland and Delaware Atlas & Gazetteer: Page 25 C5.

Description: Janes Island State Park is a great place to visit if you would like a few hours of tranquility. One could escape in the 2,900 acres of natural salt marsh, highland, and beach and encounter very few signs of civilization. It's a great place for canoes or kayaks (which can be rented at the park), as the area is usually protected from the wind and current. A good boat ramp is available, along with a large picnic area.

The fishing: The marsh and channels are more than beautiful, they are among the best fish habitat in this part of the world. They are breeding grounds and attractive to big predators because of all the bait. Fishing and crabbing are possible from the bank.

Camping and lodging: The park has 104 campsites, each with a picnic table and fire ring. Sites can accommodate tent or vehicle campers. A number of modern log cabins are available year-round; they have a six-person maximum and must be reserved in advance. The Daugherty Creek Conference Center, a 16-bed facility, can be reserved for day or overnight use as well as on a weekly basis.

For more information: Janes Island State Park; Maryland Department of Natural Resources, Fisheries Service, Eastern Region Office.

87 Crisfield

Key species: Gray trout, speckled trout, striped bass, white perch, spot, croaker, bluefish, red drum, black drum, blue crab, and flounder.

Directions: From Baltimore, take the Beltway (Interstate 695) to Interstate 97 south, then take U.S. Highway 50 east across the Bay Bridge. Continue on US 50 past Cambridge and take the Salisbury Bypass to U.S. Highway 13 south. Turn right (west) on Maryland Highway 413 and follow it to Crisfield.

DeLorme: Maryland and Delaware Atlas & Gazetteer: Page 25 C5.

Description: Many people travel to this small city just for the fishing. It is the home port of a lot of head and charter boats, and nearby Janes Island State Park offers shore-bound fishing and camping. This is also a good jumping-off point for many great fishing areas in Pocomoke and Tangier Sounds. Tangier Island and the target ships on the west side are within the small boater's range.

The fishing: Striped bass, or rockfish, usually appear in mid-April. The first fish are usually quite large, and as the spring progresses, more smaller fish show up in the mix. Most folks troll or use bait for these fish.

Croaker is the next species that becomes important, also showing up in April. Later in the season, other species such as trout, spot, flounder, Spanish mackerel, and bluefish make a run up the bay.

In the late fall, it's rockfish time again.

For more information: Maryland Department of Natural Resources, Fisheries Service, Eastern Region Office.

Delaware

Delaware is known as the First State because it was the first to ratify the Constitution, but it could be called the Millpond State because of the proliferation of these dammed-up bodies of water. In the past, many of these lakes were used to generate energy to run mills. Now they have become fish factories and produce many trophy bass, pickerel, and panfish.

Besides the millponds, Delaware has a long shoreline along the Delaware River, Delaware Bay, and the Atlantic (see the introduction to the Eastern Shore of Maryland for more information about Delaware's ocean fishing). Add all the state parks to the mix, and it makes for a state with a very diverse fishery and lots of facilities.

88 Christiana River

Key species: Largemouth bass, pickerel, bluegill, white perch, catfish, and crappie.

Directions: In Wilmington, take exit 6 from Interstate 95 and follow signs to the riverfront.

DeLorme: Maryland and Delaware Atlas & Gazetteer: Page 79 4A.

Description: This tidal river runs through downtown Wilmington. A well-developed walkway follows the bank of the stream for a long distance.

A nice Delaware Department of Natural Resources and Environmental Control (DNREC) boat ramp is located near Christiana Lake. Take I-95 to Delaware Highway 58 east (Churchmans Road) and follow it to the DNREC Boat Ramp sign on the left.

The fishing: Though very urban, this river provides excellent fishing for largemouth bass and catfish. A number of small piers are located off the walkway and are great fishing platforms. Use small live minnows for crappie, larger ones for bass. Spinnerbaits also work well here. Bluegill are caught on worms or leeches. Some anglers fly fish with small streamers for panfish.

Restrictions: At the ramp location, fishing is not allowed from the pier but bank casting is possible.

For more information: Delaware Division of Fish & Wildlife.

89 Beck's Pond

Key species: Crappie, largemouth bass, white perch, yellow perch, catfish, chain pickerel, and bluegill.

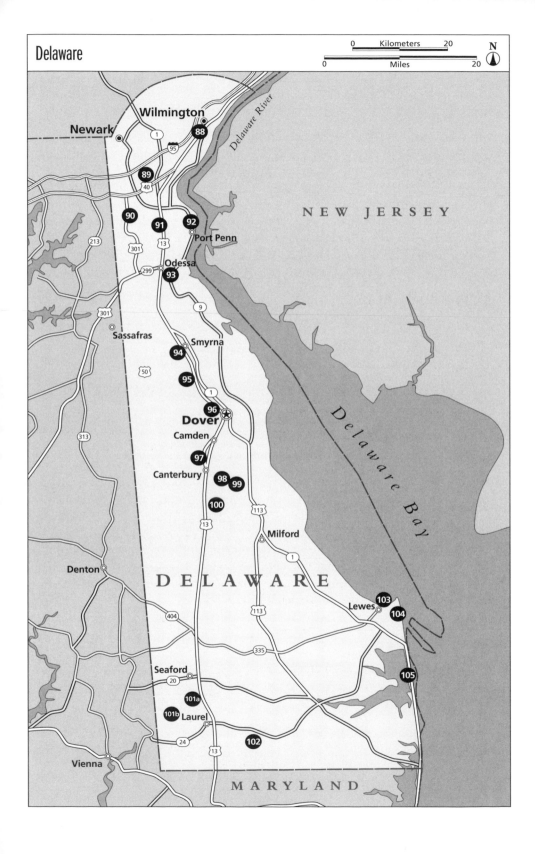

Directions: From Wilmington, take Interstate 95 south. Exit at Christiana-Stanton Road (Delaware Highway 7) south. Turn right (west) on Old Baltimore Pike, then turn left (south) on Salem Church Road and follow it to the lake on the west side of the road.

DeLorme: Maryland and Delaware Atlas & Gazetteer: Page 78 B3.

Description: Beck's Pond is a small lake: 25 acres. It's a short ride from Wilmington and a great place to take a kid fishing. A nice boat ramp is located right next to the road, and a big part of the shoreline is available for anglers.

The fishing: The big attraction here is the crappie. They are relatively easy to catch and run up to 10 inches plus. A small white jig is the preferred lure—add a small minnow for extra attraction. Bass anglers also do well at the pond. Try soft baits and spinnerbaits.

Restrictions: Gasoline engines are prohibited, but electric motors are allowed.

For more information: Delaware Division of Fish & Wildlife.

90 Lums Pond State Park

Key species: Largemouth bass, bluegill, crappie, catfish, pickerel, and striped bass.

Directions: From Wilmington, take Interstate 95 south to Delaware Highway 7. Turn right (west) on Pulaski Highway (U.S. Highway 40), then left (south) on Delaware Highway 72 (Wrangle Hill Road). Make a quick turn right (west) on Del Laws Road, then left (south) on Carvel School Road. Turn left (east) on Porter Road, then right (south) on Woods Road (Delaware Highway 402). Turn left (east) on Howell School Road, then right (south) on Buck Jersey Road and follow it to the park.

DeLorme: Maryland and Delaware Atlas & Gazetteer: Page 78 C3.

Description: The 200-acre Lums Pond is located in its namesake state park, which covers 1,790 acres. It is on the north side of the Chesapeake and Delaware Canal, which connects Chesapeake Bay and the Delaware River. A sandy beach is available for sunbathing (swimming is not allowed), and hiking trails and sports facilities are provided. Rowboats, kayaks, pedal boats, and sailboats can be rented at the concession.

The park also provides a ramp for those trailering boats. To get to the ramp, instead of turning south on Buck Jersey Road, continue east on Howell School Road to Kirkwood, then turn south on Delaware Highway 71 and follow it to the park and ramp sign.

The fishing: This is one of the finest freshwater fisheries in Delaware. Bass up to 10 pounds have been taken, and slab-size crappie are quite common. Striped bass are stocked periodically, offering an additional challenge for anglers.

Hybrid striped bass have been stocked in the past, and some are still being caught by the persistent. These fish are a cross between striped bass and white bass. They do not reproduce and have to be stocked. Most run around 5 pounds but can grow to 20 pounds.

Fish in the late evening or early morning for the hybrid striped bass. Most anglers use artificial baits that resemble silver minnows, but live minnows and night crawlers also work well.

Camping: The park offers a 68-site campground with modern showers, a dump station, picnic tables, and grills. Six of the sites have electric hookups. In addition, yurts with lots of amenities can be rented.

For more information: Lums Pond State Park; Delaware Division of Fish & Wildlife.

91 Chesapeake and Delaware Canal

Key species: Catfish, striped bass, white perch, American eel, and at times some other salty species.

The Chesapeake and Delaware Canal offers great catfishing from nice piers.

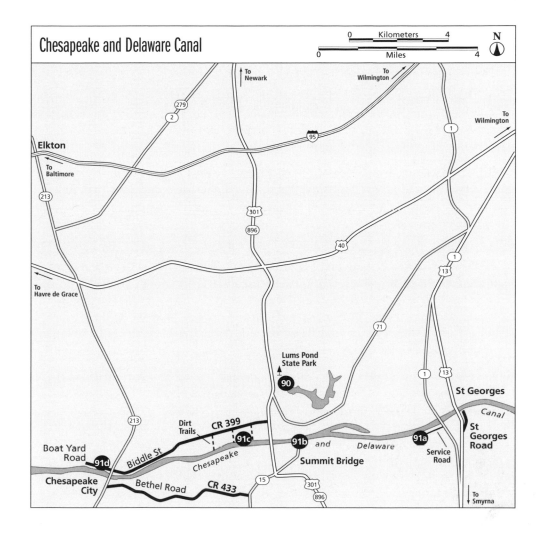

Directions: From Wilmington, take Interstate 95 south to U.S. Highway 13 south, which crosses the canal near Saint Georges.

DeLorme: *Maryland and Delaware Atlas & Gazetteer:* Page 78 C1, C2, and C3; Page 79 C4.

Accesses: Many accesses can be found along the length of the waterway. Here are a few:

91a. Exit US 13 at Saint Georges and follow Saint Georges Road south to the service road that runs along the canal. Alternatively, cross the bridge heading south, then make a very sharp turn north and follow the road to the water. The service road runs in both directions along the south bank.

91b. If you are coming south on U.S. Highway 301, cross the bridge and go east on Road 433 to Summit Bridge. Follow Road 433 through town to the canal service road.

91c. A good access can also be found on the north side of the US 301 Bridge. From Wilmington, take Interstate 95 south to US 301/Delaware Highway 896 south, then continue to Road 399 and turn either east or west. Dirt trails can be found that are drivable to the service road along the canal.

91d. In Maryland, take I-95 north from Baltimore, then turn south on Maryland Highway 213 and follow it to Chesapeake City. Biddle Street and Boat Yard Road follow the canal to the service road. You can also cross the bridge and find the service road either east or west.

Description: The Chesapeake and Delaware Canal connects Chesapeake Bay and the Delaware River. Though proposed in colonial times to connect Maryland commerce with the industrial colonies to the north, the structure wasn't completed with locks until 1829. In the 1920s, the canal was widened and lowered to sea level. Large ships still use the waterway, and it is the major seaway between Baltimore and Philadelphia. Almost all the land along its banks, both in Maryland and Delaware, is public and open for fishing.

The fishing: A fair roadway runs along both sides of the canal for most of its length. Periodically, anglers can find nice piers for use as fishing platforms. Angling is also possible from the rocks that line the banks.

The canal provides excellent fishing for catfish most of the year. Most anglers use a sliding slip sinker rig baited with either night crawlers, cut oily fish, or commercially prepared offerings.

White perch can also be caught. Use sand shrimp, bloodworms, or even small minnows. Striped bass are available, too. Try large swimming plugs or cut bait on the bottom.

For more information: Delaware Division of Fish & Wildlife.

92 Port Penn (Augustine Beach)

Key species: Striped bass, white perch, and catfish.

Directions: From Wilmington, take Interstate 95 south to U.S. Highway 13 south. In Wrangle Hill, go east on Delaware Highway 72 and follow it to Delaware Highway 9 south, which runs alongside Delaware City across the Chesapeake and Delaware Canal to Port Penn. Follow DE 9 through Port Penn to Augustine Beach.

DeLorme: Maryland and Delaware Atlas & Gazetteer: Page 79 C4.

Description: Port Penn is a sleepy little town with an extensive history. It is on the Delaware River and is part of Delaware's Coastal Heritage Greenway. A number of historic homes are located in the village.

Augustine Beach on the Delaware River is a beautiful place to surf cast.

The fishing: Augustine Beach is on the Delaware River and is a fine place to surf cast. Jetties are associated with the boat ramp and also serve as fishing platforms.

Both boat and shore anglers take advantage of a fine striped bass run in the spring. Many will bottom fish with worms. White perch can also be caught.

For more information: Delaware Division of Fish & Wildlife.

93 Appoquinimink River

Key species: Striped bass, largemouth bass, carp, catfish, white perch, and sunfish.

Directions: From Wilmington, take Interstate 95 south to U.S. Highway 13 south, which crosses the river a bit south of Odessa.

DeLorme: Maryland and Delaware Atlas & Gazetteer: Page 78 D3.

Description: The headwaters of the 10-mile-long Appoquinimink River are in eastern New Castle County about 2 miles southwest of Middletown. The stream flows more or less eastward, passing south of Odessa. It enters Delaware Bay near the mouth of the Delaware River at the Augustine Wildlife Area. A fine group, the Appoquinimink River Association, is working to keep this river clean and viable for recreational uses.

A carry-in boat ramp is located near Odessa. Turn east on Main Street (Delaware Highway 299); the ramp is on the left after passing over the bridge. Shore fishing is also possible at this location, as it is around the US 13 bridge a little south of Odessa.

The fishing: Very large carp are taken from this stream. Many anglers fish for them with canned corn kernels or homemade dough made of sugar and cornmeal. Carp will also take night crawlers, commercially prepared baits, and even flies at times.

Good striped bass fishing can be had in the spring. Many anglers cast lures and bottom fish around the Augustine Wildlife Area near Thomas Landing.

Upstream, bucketmouths are the primary targets. Big swimming plugs are popular, and some folks even fly fish for them. Large bass bugs and herring-imitating streamers work well.

For more information: Appoquinimink River Association; Delaware Division of Fish & Wildlife.

94 Lake Como

Key species: Largemouth bass, carp, bluegill, crappie, white perch, yellow perch, and chain pickerel.

Directions: From Wilmington, take Interstate 95 south to U.S. Highway 13 south. The lake is located off US 13 at the south end of Smyrna on the west side of the road.

DeLorme: Maryland and Delaware Atlas & Gazetteer: Page 62 B1.

Description: This is a well-kept and relatively productive small urban pond. A park is located right off US 13 and gives nice access to the lake. It is a great place to take a kid for a day of crappie or bluegill fishing. Nice benches are available for comfort, and a boat ramp is located in the park.

The fishing: Many folks fish from the bank in the park. Use small jigs under floats for the specks (crappie) and night crawlers for bluegill. Catfish are also popular here. Use cut oily fish, crawlers, or commercially prepared blood bait. Once in a while, a really huge channel cat is taken.

Bass fishing is also good at Como. A lot of healthy 4- to 8-pound fish are taken, and an occasional monster is brought to the net. It has been reported that Berkeley Gulp Minnows are effective here.

Fly fishing for bass and crappie is also popular. Try large bass bugs, or minnow-imitating streamers for the crappie.

Restrictions: A ramp permit is required, which may be purchased at the police department.

For more information: Delaware Division of Fish & Wildlife; fishing information, www.findthefish.com/fishingreports/svb/fishrep-svb.htm.

95 Garrison Lake

Key species: Largemouth bass, carp, bluegill, crappie, white perch, yellow perch, and chain pickerel.

Directions: From Wilmington, take Interstate 95 south to U.S. Highway 13 south. The lake is located off US 13 south of Big Oak Corner on the west side of the road.

DeLorme: Maryland and Delaware Atlas & Gazetteer: Page 62 C1.

Description: This productive pond is an 86-acre impoundment. It is a great place to take a kid for a day of crappie or bluegill fishing. A small area for the ramp is located right off US 13 and gives nice access to the lake. Boat trailer parking is limited.

The fishing: Fishing from the bank around the boat ramp is possible. Use small jigs under floats for the crappie and night crawlers for bluegill.

Big carp are present in this lake. Use corn kernels or mix your own dough with sugar and cornmeal. Commercially prepared carp baits are also excellent.

Bass anglers use an assortment of plastics on spinnerbaits as well as live minnows. Terminators, Senkos, and Sumo Frogs are used by some.

Garrison Lake is popular with families and groups.

Fly fishing for bass and crappie is also popular. Try large bass bugs, or minnow-imitating streamers for the crappie.

For more information: Delaware Division of Fish & Wildlife; fishing information, www.findthefish.com/fishingreports/svb/fishrep-svb.htm.

96 Silver Lake

Key species: Largemouth bass, carp, crappie, striped bass, white perch, chain pickerel, bluegill and other sunfish, and catfish.

Directions: From Wilmington, take Interstate 95 south to U.S. Highway 13 south to Dover. Follow US 13 through town and turn right (west) on White Oak Road. Turn right (north) at the City of Dover Park sign and drive to the lake and boat ramp.

Silver Lake, a well-managed urban lake with a nice boat ramp and picnic tables, makes a fine fishing destination.

DeLorme: Maryland and Delaware Atlas & Gazetteer: Page 62 D1.

Description: This is a well-managed urban lake in a nice park with picnic benches and a boat ramp.

The fishing: Crankbaits are very effective here. Many anglers also use plastics and spinnerbaits. When the fish are deep, as in midsummer during the day, try deep-diving plugs and jigs. Terminators, Senkos, and Sumo Frogs are used by some.

Popular fly patterns for bass are deer hair frogs, large popper bugs, hairy crawfish, large silvery streamers, and diving bass bugs in chartreuse. For bluegill, try bream busters, bee poppers in various colors, weedless divers, and small silvery streamers.

Restrictions: A permit from the City of Dover Parks and Recreation Department is required to fish in Silver Lake.

For more information: Delaware Division of Fish & Wildlife; fishing information, www.findthefish.com/fishingreports/svb/fishrep-svb.htm; City of Dover Parks and Recreation Department.

97 Derby Pond

Key species: Largemouth bass, bluegill, yellow perch, chain pickerel, crappie, and catfish.

Directions: From Wilmington, take Interstate 95 south to U.S. Highway 13 south and pass through Dover. In Camden, turn right (west) on Alternate US 13 and proceed south to the pond on the right.

DeLorme: Maryland and Delaware Atlas & Gazetteer: Page 52 A1.

Description: This is a small pond with an acceptable ramp but very limited parking.

The fishing: Derby Pond is a typical bluegill/crappie/largemouth water. Night crawlers work well for bucketmouths and bluegill.

Fly fishing for bluegill could provide plenty of action. Try bream busters, bee poppers in various colors, weedless divers, and small silvery streamers. Mosquito and gnat patterns also work well here.

For more information: Delaware Division of Fish & Wildlife.

98 McGinnis Pond

Key species: Largemouth bass, bluegill, carp, crappie, white perch, chain pickerel, and catfish.

Directions: From Wilmington, take Interstate 95 south to U.S. Highway 13 south. Pass through Dover, then Camden. At Plymouth, turn left (east) on Plymouth

Road, which becomes Barretts Chapel Road. Turn right (south) on McGinnis Pond Road and follow it to the lake on the west side of the road.

DeLorme: Maryland and Delaware Atlas & Gazetteer: Page 52 B1.

Description: This is an old millpond located near Lexington Mill. It has a decent ramp but not much parking for trailers.

The fishing: McGinnis Pond is another typical bluegill/crappie/largemouth water. Night crawlers work well for bucketmouths and bluegill.

Fly fishing for bass and bluegill is a definite possibility. Big bass bugs are a favorite, as are poppers. Streamers resembling shiners are effective, too. Also try bream busters, bee poppers in various colors, weedless divers, and mosquito and gnat patterns.

For more information: Delaware Division of Fish & Wildlife.

99 Andrews Lake

Key species: Largemouth bass, bluegill, crappie, white perch, yellow perch, chain pickerel, and catfish.

Directions: From Wilmington, take Interstate 95 south to U.S. Highway 13 south. Pass through Dover, then Camden. South of Plymouth, turn left (east) on Andrews Lake Road (Delaware Highway 380) and follow it to the lake and ramp on the west side of the road.

DeLorme: Maryland and Delaware Atlas & Gazetteer: Page 52 B2.

Description: This small pond near Lexington Mill has an acceptable ramp but very limited parking.

The fishing: Andrews Lake is a typical bluegill/crappie/largemouth water. Night crawlers work well for bucketmouths and bluegill.

Fly fishing for bluegill could provide plenty of action. Try bream busters, bee poppers in various colors, weedless divers, and small silvery streamers. Mosquito and gnat patterns also work well here.

For more information: Delaware Division of Fish & Wildlife.

100 Killens Pond State Park

Key species: Largemouth bass, bluegill and other sunfish, carp, catfish, crappie, white perch, and chain pickerel.

Directions: From Wilmington, take Interstate 95 south to U.S. Highway 13 south. Pass through Dover, Camden, and Plymouth to a left (east) on Johnnycake Landing Road (County Road 34). Turn right (south) on Chimney Hill Road (County Road

385), then turn left (east) on Killens Pond Road and follow it to the ramp and parking area on the lake.

DeLorme: Maryland and Delaware Atlas & Gazetteer: Page 52 B1.

Description: Natural and recreational opportunities abound at Killens Pond State Park, centrally located in the heart of Kent County. The park's centerpiece is the 66-acre millpond, which features boating and fishing. It's a great place to introduce a kid to fishing.

The millpond was established in the late 1700s. Prior to the pond's creation, the Murderkill River and surrounding hardwood forest were home to several Native American settlements and hunting camps. According to legend, the river's unusual name refers to a local tribe's massacre of a Dutch trading party at the mouth of the river in 1648. Now a peaceful oasis, Killens Pond became a state park in 1965.

A fishing pier is available at the park. Canoes, rowboats, surf bikes, kayaks, and pedal boats can be rented during the summer.

The fishing: There is good fishing in this old millpond for bass, crappie, and pickerel. Some very large carp are present for those who want to try for them. Bluegill run up to 8 inches and crappie up to 10 inches.

Camping and lodging: The wooded campground is a popular attraction at Killens Pond. This year-round facility boasts 59 sites, with electric and water hookups, accommodating both tents and RVs. In addition, there is a primitive camping loop for tents only, which features 17 beautiful secluded sites.

The park also offers camping cabins that sleep four and feature an efficiency kitchen with an eating area, bedroom, bath with shower, air-conditioning, and heat. A picnic table, grill, and porch are located outside. Subject to availability, cabin rentals include the use of a canoe and rowboats.

For more information: Killens Pond State Park; Delaware Division of Fish & Wildlife.

101 Nanticoke River, Delaware

Key species: Largemouth bass, sunfish, various catfish species, crappie, white perch, yellow perch, and chain pickerel.

Directions: From Wilmington, take Interstate 95 south to U.S. Highway 13 south to Seaford.

DeLorme: Maryland and Delaware Atlas & Gazetteer: Page 44 C1.

Accesses: **101a, Seaford Ramps.** From US 13 south, turn right (west) on Delaware Highway 20 and follow it through Seaford. Turn left (south) on Shipley Street and follow it to the ramps.

101b, Phillips Landing. From US 13 south of Seaford, take Road 485 southwest to Bethel. At Shell Bridge, turn right (west) on Road 493 and follow it through Portsville. Take the second right after passing Portsville Pond and follow the signs to Phillips Landing.

Description: The Nanticoke River runs for a long distance through Delaware before crossing into Maryland near the town of Galestown. The headwaters are in Sussex County, then the river widens in Kent County just as it passes near the city of Seaford. Numerous fishing opportunities present themselves for the entire length of this stream.

The fishing: This river sustains the heaviest fishing pressure of all tidal streams in Delaware, with most anglers seeking the resident largemouth bass. The Nanticoke was once one of the most productive fisheries for American shad. Since their numbers have greatly decreased, it is not legal to keep any at the present time.

The entire river is excellent largemouth bass, crappie, bluegill, and catfish habitat. White perch fishing is excellent in the spring, but some can be caught throughout the year.

Catfish are available throughout the river and are caught by using either cut fish or commercially prepared stink baits. Bass anglers can have a ball on the Nanticoke, and a wide variety of sizes can be taken. Broad Creek is an excellent bucketmouth location. Fish both the creek mouth as well as upstream from there. This area can be accessed by boat from Phillips Landing.

The docks around Seaford also hold plenty of bass as well as crappie. Many anglers like to fish the pilings around the Woodland Ferry. Some of the favorite lures are buzzbaits, spinnerbaits, and small plastic worms. Swimming plugs are also effective. Fly fishers do well here, too. Try big bass bugs and poppers, or small streamers for the crappie.

Shore-bound anglers can also enjoy the Nanticoke. The docks at the ramps in Seaford are easily accessible, and the bank by Phillips Landing is also popular. Many good catfish are taken here.

Restrictions: No license is needed in Delaware to fish in tidewater, but always check the current regulations with the Division of Fish & Wildlife to be sure this has not changed.

For more information: Delaware Division of Fish & Wildlife.

102 Trap Pond State Park

Key species: Largemouth bass, crappie, bluegill, catfish, yellow perch, and chain pickerel.

Directions: From Wilmington, take Interstate 95 south to U.S. Highway 13 south and pass through Dover, Camden, and Seaford. In Laurel, turn left (east) on

Delaware Highway 24, then right (south) on Road 463. At Lowe, turn left (east) on Road 449 and follow it to the park and lake.

DeLorme: Maryland and Delaware Atlas & Gazetteer: Page 44 D2.

Description: Trap Pond covers 90 acres, and the park is 3,100 acres. A year-round nature center with programs, trails, and a playground can provide entertainment when you are not fishing. This park is home to the northernmost stand of bald cypress trees in the United States.

Canoe, kayak, pedal boat, and rowboat rentals are available. A ramp to launch small boats can be used by visitors.

The fishing: Some nice bucketmouths inhabit Trap Pond. Bluegill are plentiful and provide sport for kids and adults alike. Fly fishing for both these species is possible here.

Hiking trails surround the lake and give many accesses for shore-bound anglers.

Camping and lodging: The park has 142 lakeside campsites, 130 of which have water and electric hookups, located in a stand of loblolly pines. Two primitive camping areas for groups are available by reservation only. Camping cabins and yurts are also available.

For more information: Trap Pond State Park; Delaware Division of Fish & Wildlife.

103 Lewes

Key species: Striped bass, gray trout (weakfish), sea bass, black drum, tautog (blackfish), summer flounder (fluke), bluefish, croaker, spot, red drum, offshore tuna, bonita, wahoo, king mackerel, Spanish mackerel, and dolphin.

Directions: From Wilmington, take Interstate 95 south to Delaware Highway 1 south to U.S. Highway 9 northeast to Lewes.

From Baltimore, take the Beltway (Interstate 695) to Interstate 97 south. In Annapolis, take U.S. Highway 50 east across the Bay Bridge to Wye Mills, then go east on Maryland Highway 404, which takes you to Delaware and merges with US 9 in Georgetown. Follow US 9 to Lewes.

DeLorme: Maryland and Delaware Atlas & Gazetteer: Page 45 A6.

Description: Lewes is a small city, and sport fishing is a major part of its economy. Many motels and hotels are available, and camping is possible nearby in Cape Henlopen State Park as well as many private campgrounds. All amenities are located within or right outside the city limits.

The fishing: Whether you enjoy fishing from the beach, rocks, or pier, or charter, head, or private boats, Lewes has it all. The fishing starts in winter, with boats heading out to the offshore reefs and wrecks in search of tautog. April usually sees the first inshore 'tog caught from rocks and other obstructions.

As the season progresses, in April or May sea bass begin to show up, and surf casters, pier anglers, and trollers soon begin to pick up striped bass and bluefish. Flounder begin their annual run in late April or May, and weakfish also make an appearance at this time.

In May, big black drum make a run up the shore toward Delaware Bay.

June through late November is prime time for offshore anglers. The blue-water folks catch tuna, bonita, wahoo, white and blue marlin, king mackerel, and an occasional swordfish.

The best fishing of the year takes place in autumn. Most of the species previously mentioned feed heavily before their annual offshore and southward migrations. It then winds up as it began, with great 'tog fishing on the offshore wrecks beginning in December.

For more information: Delaware Division of Fish & Wildlife.

104 Cape Henlopen State Park

Key species: Striped bass, bluefish, kingfish (whiting), spot, croaker, red drum, and flounder.

Directions: From Wilmington, take Interstate 95 south to Delaware Highway 1 south. Follow DE 1 past Dover and Milford to U.S. Highway 9 east. Take US 9 to Lewes, then follow the signs to the park.

From Baltimore, take the Beltway (Interstate 695) to Interstate 97 south. In Annapolis, take U.S. Highway 50 east across the Bay Bridge to Wye Mills, then go east on Maryland Highway 404, which takes you to Delaware and merges with U.S. Highway 9 in Georgetown. Take US 9 to Lewes and follow the signs to the park.

DeLorme: Maryland and Delaware Atlas & Gazetteer: Page 45 A6.

Description: This is one of Delaware's premier state parks on the ocean. It is quite large and offers most amenities and lots of activities for those who do not fish.

The fishing: The park boasts a quarter-mile-long pier jutting out into Delaware Bay. Bait and tackle are available at the pier as well as fishing supplies and snack foods. Transportation along the pier for the disabled is available April through October.

For those who prefer surf fishing, the park's ocean beaches are open year-round. Walkways across dunes give access to pedestrian and vehicle traffic.

Restrictions: Delaware's regulations on size and bag limit for marine species change often, so make sure you check before heading out. Only surf anglers are allowed to drive onto the beach, and a special permit is required. Permits are available online or at the park office. Wheeled travel on the beach is highly restricted; see www .destateparks.com/know/rules/rules.htm#7.1 for details.

Camping: The park has 150 spacious campsites located on the pine-covered dunes, and most have water hookups. Camping is available March through November.

For more information: Cape Henlopen State Park; Delaware Division of Fish & Wildlife.

105 Delaware Seashore State Park

Key species: Striped bass, bluefish, tautog, kingfish (whiting), spotted trout, gray trout (weakfish), spot, croaker, red drum, and flounder.

Directions: From Wilmington, take Interstate 95 south to Delaware Highway 1 south and follow it past Dover and Milford. Continue on DE 1 to the coast, where the road turns south. The park starts south of Indian Beach and runs past the Indian River inlet.

From Baltimore, take the Beltway (Interstate 695) to Interstate 97 south. In Annapolis, take U.S. Highway 50 east across the Bay Bridge to Wye Mills, then go east on Maryland Highway 404 through Georgetown. At Five Points, turn southeast on DE 1 and continue to the coast, where the road turns south. The park starts south of Indian Beach and runs past the Indian River inlet.

DeLorme: Maryland and Delaware Atlas & Gazetteer: Page 45 B6 and C6.

Description: With 6 miles of ocean and bay shoreline, Delaware Seashore State Park covers 2,825 acres. It has shoreline on the Atlantic, Rehoboth Bay, and Indian River Bay.

The jetties at the Indian River inlet are in this park. For those trailering a boat, a ramp is located on the northwest side of the bridge over the inlet.

The fishing: Three types of shore-bound angling is available from the park, and some of the best surf casting on the entire East Coast takes place here. Everything from blues and stripers to croaker, spot, and kingfish are available to persistent anglers.

The jetties on both sides of the Indian River inlet provide excellent platforms for casters. Besides the species mentioned for surf casters, tautog, shad, and herring can also be caught from the rocks at certain times of the year.

The Rehoboth Bay side of the barrier beaches also offers opportunities for salt anglers. Footpaths to the water provide access. Bluefish, flounder, and weakfish may be caught from the shore. The trout bite best at night. Try soft-tail grubs or metal jigs.

Besides land-based fishing, Indian Inlet Marina and Lewes have a great assortment of both head and charter boats. You can take off for a day of inshore bottom-bouncing for sea bass, tautog, flounder, and/or weakfish or an offshore adventure for the blue-water species: tuna, wahoo, king mackerel, bonita, etc.

Restrictions: Delaware's regulations on size and bag limit for marine species change often, so make sure you check before heading out. Only surf anglers are allowed to drive onto the beach, and a special permit is required. Wheeled travel on the beach is highly restricted; see www.destateparks.com/know/rules/rules.htm#7.1 for details.

Camping: This park has a nice campground. Some sites have hookups. Call for information.

For more information: Delaware Seashore State Park; Delaware Division of Fish & Wildlife; tide information, www.beach-net.com/TidesIR.html.

Appendix A: Trout Streams in Maryland

Some of the streams run through more than one county. In these instances, only one is listed. Always check current regulations, as boundaries may change.

Allegany County

Evitts Creek	Around Dickens, upstream of Interstate 68
Fifteen Mile Creek	North of Little Orleans
Flintstone Creek	Around Flintstone
George's Creek	Around Gilmore
Jennings Run	Around Mount Savage, parallels Maryland Highway 36
North Branch Jennings Run	North of Barrelville
Sidling Hill Creek	Pennsylvania state line to Pearre Road
Town Creek	Main stem, near Maryland Highway 51
Wills Creek	From Braddock Run to state line

Anne Arundel County

Severn Run Watershed	Upstream of Maryland Highway 3

Baltimore County

Beetree Run	Bentley Springs upstream
Dead Run	The main stem
Gunpowder Falls	From Monkton to Prettyboy Dam
Gwynns Falls	South of Maryland Highway 140
Jones Falls Watershed	North of the Beltway (Interstate 695)
Little Falls Watershed	From Graystone upstream
Little Gunpowder Falls	Border of Harford County
Patapsco River	From Blodes Dam downstream to B&O viaduct

Carroll County

Beaver Run	Near Finksburg, north of Maryland Highway 91
Morgan Run	Around Klee Mill
Piney Run	From bridge on Arrington Road to confluence with South Branch
South Branch Patapsco River	From confluence of North Branch to Maryland Highway 32, Sykesville

Cecil County

Basin Run Watershed — Liberty Grove area
Principio Creek Watershed — Upstream of Maryland Highway 7

City of Baltimore

Herring Run — In the city

Frederick County

Carroll Creek — Frederick
Fishing Creek Watershed — North of Fishing Creek Reservoir
Friends Creek — Near Friends Creek
Hunting Creek Watershed — Near Cunningham Falls State Park
Little Hunting Creek Watershed — Upstream of U.S. Highway 15 near Catoctin
Middle Creek Watershed — Upstream of Ellerton
Owens Creek — Upstream of US 15

Garrett County

Bear Creek Watershed — Around Kaese Mill, parallels Bear Creek Road
Buffalo Run Watershed — Near Sand Spring, parallels Buffalo Run Road
Casselman River — Near Grantsville, from U.S. Highway 40 to Pennsylvania
Herrington Creek — Near Herrington Manor State Park
Laurel Run — Along Laurel Run Cemetery Road
Little Youghiogheny River — Near Oakland, downstream from U.S. Highway 219
Mill Run Watershed — Upstream of Youghiogheny River Lake
Muddy Creek — From Youghiogheny River to Cranesville Road
North Branch Potomac — West Virginia border
Salt Block Run — Off White Rock Road
Savage River Watershed — All of it except New Germany Lake
Youghiogheny River — Upstream of Maryland Highway 42

Harford County

Deer Creek   Near Rocks State Park

Montgomery County

Cabin Branch   Upstream from near Annapolis Rock,
                                    upstream to Hipsley Mill Road
Great Seneca Creek   Around Seneca Creek State Park
Little Seneca Creek   From Little Seneca Lake to Maryland
                                    Highway 28
Northwest Branch   Near Cloverly
Paint Branch   Above Fairland Road, all tributaries
Patuxent River   From Maryland Highway 27 downstream
                                    to Maryland Highway 97

Prince Georges County

Patuxent River   Around Laurel

Washington County

Beaver Creek   Near Breathedsville, upstream of Interstate 68
Little Antietam Creek   From the mouth to Dogstreet Bridge
Little Tonoloway Creek   Section in Weidmeyer Park

Appendix B: Trout Waters in Delaware

Trout fishing in Delaware is basically a put-and-take fishery, supported by trout stamps. Some special regulations apply, so check before you fish. There is a two-week closure of all fishing in trout streams prior to the opening day of spring trout season. Trout-fishing hours are a half hour before sunrise to one hour after sunset, except on opening day, when fishing begins at 7:30 a.m. The daily limit is six in possession. After the six-fish limit is reached, you are not allowed to fish in designated trout streams during that day.

In some restricted trout streams or portions of streams, it is only legal to fish with fly rods and artificial flies. Flies may only have a single-point hook, with no more than two flies on a line. Any other lures or bait are prohibited. A four-fish limit is in place on restricted streams.

The above are just a few of the current regulations, and they periodically change. Be sure to check with the Department of Natural Resources Division of Fish & Wildlife for current information.

Kent County

Tidbury Pond	Stocked pond

New Castle County

Beaver Run	Pennsylvania state line to Brandywine River
Christina Creek	Maryland state line to Rittenhouse Park
Mill Creek	Maryland Highway 7 to Brackenville Road
Pike Creek	Maryland Highway 72 to Henderson Road
White Clay Creek	Paper Mill Road to the Pennsylvania state line, part of which is fly fishing only (check regulations)
Wilson Run	Brandywine Creek State Park to Maryland Highway 72

Sussex County

Blockhouse Pond	In Lewes

Appendix C: For More Information

Government Offices and Agencies

Baltimore County Department of
  Recreation and Parks
301 Washington Avenue, Mailstop 52
Towson, Maryland 21204
(410) 887-3871
(410) 887-5319 (TTY)
www.co.ba.md.us/agencies/recreation

Bowie City Hall
2614 Kenhill Drive
Bowie, MD 20715
(301) 262-6200
(301) 809-5013 (TTY)

Caroline County Recreation & Parks
403 South Seventh Street, Suite 226
Denton, MD 21629
(410) 479-8120
www.carolinerecreation.org

Charles County Department of
  Public Facilities
10430 Audie Lane
P.O. Box 1050
LaPlata, Maryland 20646
(301) 932-3440 or (301) 870-2778
www.charlescounty.org/pf/pg/parks/
  pavrent.htm

City of Baltimore Reservoir Natural
  Resources Office
5685 Oakland Road
Eldersburg, MD 21784-6828
(410) 795-6151
http://baltimorecity.gov/government/
  dpw/reservoirs.php

DC Department of Health
Fisheries and Wildlife Division
51 N Street NE, Fifth Floor
Washington, DC 20002
(800) ASK-FISH
http://app.doh.dc.gov/services/
  administration_offices/environmental/
  services2/fishers_wildlife/angler_
  hotline.shtm

Delaware Division of Fish & Wildlife
89 Kings Highway
Dover, DE 19901
(302) 739-9910
www.fw.delaware.gov/fisheries

Dover Parks and Recreation
  Department
Dover City Hall
15 East Loockerman Street
Dover, DE 19903
(302) 736-7050

Havre de Grace City Yacht Basin
352 Commerce Street
Havre de Grace, MD 21078
(410) 939-0015

Howard County Recreation and Parks
7120 Oakland Mills Road
Columbia, MD 21046-1677
(410) 313-4700
www.co.ho.md.us/rap

Kent County Parks and Recreation
10932 Worton Road
P.O. Box 67
Worton, MD 21678
(410) 778-1948
www.kentparksandrec.org

Laurel Parks & Recreation Department
8103 Sandy Spring Road
Laurel, MD 20707
(301) 725-7800
www.laurel.md.us/parks.htm

Maryland Department of Natural
  Resources
Fisheries Service
www.dnr.state.md.us/fisheries

> Cedarville Visitor's Center
> Maryland Highway 4, Box 106E
> Brandywine, MD 20613
> (301) 888-2423

> Central Region Office
> 17400 Annapolis Rock Road
> Woodbine, Maryland 21797
> (410) 442-2080

> Eastern Region Office
> 14214 Old Wye Mills Road
> Wye Mills, MD 21679
> (410) 827-6245

> Lewistown Work Center
> 10932 Putman Road
> Thurmont, MD 21788
> (301) 898-9724

> Rivers and Reservoirs Project
> (301) 898-9724

> Western Region Office
> 1728 Kings Run Road
> Oakland, MD 21550
> (301) 334-8218

Maryland Department of Natural
  Resources
Wildlife & Heritage Service
www.dnr.state.md.us/wildlife

> Bel Air Regional Office
> 2 South Bond Street
> Bel Air, MD 21014
> (410) 836-4557 (local)
> (410) 879-4500, ext. 4557
> (Baltimore)

> Prince Frederick Office
> 6904 Hallowing Lane
> Prince Frederick, MD 20678
> (410) 535-0282

> Salisbury Office
> 201 Baptist Street, Suite 22
> Salisbury, MD 21801
> (410) 543-6795

Maryland Greenways Commission
580 Taylor Avenue, E-2
Annapolis, MD 21401
(410) 260-8780
www.dnr.state.md.us/greenways

Montgomery County Department
  of Parks
9500 Brunett Avenue
Silver Spring, MD 20901
(301) 495-2595
www.montgomeryparks.org

Perryville Town Hall
515 Broad Street
P.O. Box 773
Perryville, MD 21903
(410) 642-6066

US Army Corps of Engineers

Baltimore District (Jennings
Randolph Lake)
P.O. Box 1715
Baltimore, MD 21203-1715
(410) 962-7608
www.nab.usace.army.mil/
recreation/jenran.htm

Pittsburgh District (Youghiogheny
River Lake)
497 Flanigan Road
Confluence, PA 15424-1902
(814) 395-3242
(814) 395-3166 (daily lake and
recreation information)
www.lrp.usace.army.mil/rec/lakes/
youghiog.htm

U.S. Fish and Wildlife Service
National Wildlife Visitor Center
10901 Scarlet Tanager Loop
Laurel, MD 20708-4027
(301) 497-5760

Washington Suburban Sanitary
Commission
14501 Sweitzer Lane
Laurel, MD 20707
(301) 206-9772 or (800) 828-6439
www.wssc.dst.md.us/info/watershed
.cfm

Chambers of Commerce, Tourism Offices, and Associations

Annapolis and Anne Arundel County
Chamber of Commerce
49 Old Solomons Road, Suite 204
Annapolis, MD 21401
(410) 266-3960

Appoquinimink River Association
P.O. Box 341
Middletown, DE 19709
(302) 382-0335
http://water19709.web.aplus.net

Calvert County Chamber of
Commerce
P.O. Box 9
Prince Frederick, MD 20678-0009
(410) 535-2577
(301) 855-1930 (DC Metro)

Chester River Association
100 North Cross Street, Suite 1
Chestertown, MD 21620
(410) 810-7556
www.chesterriverassociation.org

Dorchester County Department
of Tourism
2 Rose Hill Place
Cambridge, MD 21613
(410) 228-1000 or (800) 522-TOUR
www.tourdorchester.org

Garrett County Chamber of
Commerce
15 Visitors Center Drive
McHenry, MD 21541
www.garrettchamber.com

Havre de Grace Office of Tourism and
    Visitor Center
450 Pennington Avenue
Havre de Grace, MD 21078
(410) 939-21001 or (800) 851-7756
www.hdgtourism.com

Kent County Tourism Development
    Office
400 High Street
Chestertown, MD 21620
(410) 778-0416
www.kentcounty.com/tourism

Prettyboy Watershed Alliance
21619 Gunpowder Road
Lineboro, MD 21102
(410) 239-0640

Roland E. Powell Convention Center
4001 Coastal Highway
Ocean City, MD 21842
(800) 626-2326
www.ococean.com

Sassafras River Association
P.O. Box 333
Georgetown, MD 21930
(410) 648-6994

St. Mary's County Chamber of
    Commerce
44200 Airport Road
California, MD 20619
(301) 737-3001

Parks, Forests, and Natural Areas

Anacostia Park
1900 Anacostia Drive SE
Washington, DC 20020
(202) 472-3873

Assateague State Park
7307 Stephen Decatur Highway
Berlin, MD 21811
(410) 641-2120
(888) 432-CAMP (2267) (reservations)
www.dnr.state.md.us/publiclands/
    eastern/assateague.html

Big Run State Park
c/o New Germany State Park
349 Headquarters Lane
Grantsville, MD 21536
(301) 895-5453
www.dnr.state.md.us/publiclands/
    western/newgermany.html

Blackwater National Wildlife Refuge
2145 Key Wallace Drive
Cambridge, MD 21613
(410) 228-2677

Cape Henlopen State Park
42 Cape Henlopen Drive
Lewes, DE 19958
(302) 645-8983
(302) 645-2103 (campground)
www.destateparks.com/chsp/chsp.htm

Catoctin Mountain (National) Park
6602 Foxville Road
Thurmont, MD 21788
(301) 663-9330 (headquarters)
(301) 663-9388 (visitor center)
www.nps.gov/cato

Cedar Haven Fishing Area
18400 Phyllis Weatley Boulevard
Eagle Harbor, MD 20608
(301) 627-6074
(301) 669-2544 (TTY)

Cosca Regional Park
11000 Thrift Road
Clinton, MD 20735
General information: (301) 868-1397;
(301) 203-6030 (TTY)
Clearwater Nature Center:
   (301) 297-4575; (301) 699-2544 (TTY)

Cunningham Falls State Park
14039 Catoctin Hollow Road
Thurmont, MD 21788
(301) 271-7574
(888) 432-CAMP (2267) (reservations)
www.dnr.state.md.us/publiclands/
   western/cunninghamfalls.html

Deep Creek Lake State Park
898 State Park Road
Swanton, MD 21561
(301) 387-5563
(888) 432-CAMP (2267) (reservations)
www.dnr.state.md.us/publiclands/
   western/deepcreeklake.html

Delaware Seashore State Park
130 Coastal Highway
Rehoboth Beach, DE 19971
(302) 227-2800
(302) 539-7202 (campground)
www.destateparks.com/dssp/dssp.asp

Fort Washington (National) Park
13551 Fort Washington Road
Fort Washington, MD 20744
(301) 763-4600
www.nps.gov/fowa

Gilbert Run Park
13140 Charles Street
Charlotte Hall, MD 20622
(301) 932-1083
http://somd.com/detailed/1519.php

Governor's Bridge Natural Area and
   Canoe Launch
7600 Governor's Bridge Road
Bowie, MD 20716
(301) 627-6074
(301) 699-2544 (TTY)
www.pgparks.com/places/parks/
   governor.html

Greenbrier State Park
21843 National Pike
Boonsboro, MD 21713-9535
(301) 791-4767
(888) 432-CAMP (2267) (reservations)
www.dnr.state.md.us/publiclands/
   western/greenbrier.html

Green Ridge State Forest
28700 Headquarters Drive NE
Flintstone, MD 21530-9525
(301) 478-3124
www.dnr.state.md.us/publiclands/
   western/greenridge.html

Greenwell State Park
25420 Rosedale Manor Lane
Hollywood, MD 20636
(301) 373-9775
www.dnr.state.md.us/publiclands/
   southern/greenwell.html

Janes Island State Park
26280 Alfred Lawson Drive
Crisfield, MD 21817
(410) 968-1565
(888) 432-CAMP (2267) (reservations)
www.dnr.state.md.us/publiclands/
   eastern/janesisland.html

Lake Artemesia Natural Area
Branchview/Ballew Avenue
Berwyn Heights, MD 29740
(301) 927-2163
(301) 699-2544 (TTY)

Killens Pond State Park
5025 Killens Pond Road
Felton, DE 19943
(302) 284-4526
(302) 284-3412 (campground)
www.destateparks.com/kpsp/kpsp.htm

Lums Pond State Park
1068 Howell School Road
Bear, DE 19701
(302) 368-6989
www.destateparks.com/lpsp/lpsp.asp

Martinak State Park
137 Deep Shore Road
Denton, MD 21629
(410) 820-1668
(888) 432-CAMP (2267) (reservations)
www.dnr.state.md.us/publiclands/
    eastern/martinak.html

Patapsco Valley State Park
8020 Baltimore National Pike
Ellicott City, MD 21043
(410) 461-5005
(888) 432-CAMP (2267) (reservations)
www.dnr.state.md.us/publiclands/
    central/patapscovalley.html

Patuxent River Park
16000 Croom Airport Road
Upper Marlboro, MD 20772
(301) 627-6074
(301) 699-2544 (TTY)
www.pgparks.com/places/parks/
    patuxent.html

Patuxent River State Park
c/o Seneca Creek State Park
11950 Clopper Road
Gaithersburg, MD 20878
(301) 924-2127
www.dnr.state.md.us/publiclands/
    central/patuxentriver.html

Piney Run Park
30 Martz Road
Sykesville, MD 21784
(410) 795-3274
www.cygnuswinecellars.com/cellar/
    pineyrun.html

Piscataway (National) Park
13551 Fort Washington Road
Fort Washington, MD 20744
(301) 763-4600 (management
information)
(301) 283-2113 (visitor center)
www.nps.gov/pisc

Point Lookout State Park
11175 Point Lookout Road
Scotland, MD 20687
(301) 872-5688
(888) 432-CAMP (2267) (reservations)
www.dnr.state.md.us/publiclands/
    southern/pointlookout.html

Potomac State Forest
1431 Potomac Camp Road
Oakland, MD 21550
(301) 334-2038
www.dnr.state.md.us/publiclands/
    western/potomacforest.html

Queen Anne Fishing Area and
    Canoe Launch
18700 Queen Anne Bridge Road
Upper Marlboro, MD 20774
(301) 627-6074
(301) 699-2544 (TTY)

Rock Creek Regional Park (Lake
    Needwood)
15700 Needwood Lake Circle
Rockville, MD 20847
(301) 762-9500
www.nps.gov/rocr

Rocks State Park
3318 Rocks Chrome Hill Road
Jarrettsville, MD 21084
(410) 557-7994
(888) 432-CAMP (2267)
(pavilion reservations)
www.dnr.state.md.us/publiclands/
    central/rocks.html

Rocky Gap State Park
Maryland Highway 1, Box 90
Flintstone, MD 21530
(301) 722-1480
(888) 432-CAMP (2267) (reservations)
www.dnr.state.md.us/publiclands/
    western/rockygap.html

Sandy Point State Park
1100 East College Parkway
Annapolis, MD 21401
(410) 974-2149
(888) 432-CAMP (2267) (reservations)
www.dnr.state.md.us/publiclands/
    southern/sandypoint.html

Savage River State Forest
127 Headquarters Lane
Grantsville, MD 21536
(301) 895-5759
www.dnr.state.md.us/publiclands/
    western/savageriver.html

Seneca Creek State Park
11950 Clopper Road
Gaithersburg, MD 20878
(301) 924-2127
(888) 432-CAMP (2267) (reservations)
www.dnr.state.md.us/publiclands/
    central/seneca.html

Smallwood State Park
2750 Sweden Point Road
Marbury, MD 20658
(301) 743-7613
(888) 432-CAMP (2267) (reservations)
www.dnr.state.md.us/publiclands/
    southern/smallwood.html

St. Mary's River State Park
c/o Point Lookout State Park
11175 Point Lookout Road
Scotland, MD 20687
(301) 872-5688
www.dnr.state.md.us/publiclands/
    southern/stmarysriver.html

Susquehanna State Park
c/o Rocks State Park
3318 Rocks Chrome Hill Road
Jarrettsville, MD 21084
(410) 557-7994
(888) 432-CAMP (2267) (reservations)
www.dnr.state.md.us/publiclands/
    central/susquehanna.html

Trap Pond State Park
33587 Bald Cypress Lane
Laurel, DE 19956
(302) 875-5153
(302) 875-2392 (campground)
(302) 875-5163 (nature center)
www.destateparks.com/tpsp/tpsp.htm

Tuckahoe State Park
13070 Crouse Mill Road
Queen Anne, MD 21657
(410) 820-1668
www.dnr.state.md.us/publiclands/
    eastern/tuckahoe.html

Tackle and Fly Shops and Marinas

Western Maryland

Bassin Box
1068 National Highway
Lavale, MD 21502
(301) 729-4088

BJ's
11329 Savage River Road
Swanton, MD 21561
(301) 777-0001
bjsjim@mindspring.com

Deep Creek Outfitters
32 Outfitters Way
McHenry, MD 21541
(301) 387-2200

Fox's Sport & Bait Shop
501 South Market Street
Frederick, MD 21701
(301) 663-3697

Keystone Sporting Goods Inc.
13611 Pennsylvania Avenue
Hagerstown, MD 21742
(301) 733-0373

Reels & Wheels
17328 Taylors Landing Road
Sharpsburg, MD 21782
(301) 432-7281

Spring Creek Outfitters
578 Deep Creek Drive
McHenry, MD 21541
(301) 387-2034

Thurmont Sporting Goods
4 East Main Street
Thurmont, MD 21788
(301) 271-7404

Wolfe's on the Square
1 West Potomac Street
Williamsport, MD 21795
(301) 223-7411

Northeastern Maryland

Anglers Hollow
34 West Main Street
Westminster, MD 21157
(410) 751-9349

Anglers Lie
2100 North Glebe Road
Arlington, VA 22207
(703) 527-2524

Anglers Sport Center Limited
1456 Whitehall Road
Annapolis, MD 21401
(410) 974-4013

Backwoods Sports
514 Pulaski Highway
Joppa, MD 21085
(410) 679-7871

Bay Pro Shop
2855 Chesapeake Beach Road
Dunkirk, MD 20754
(301) 855-0351
www.chesapeake.net/baypro

Beck's Gunsmithing
19200 Middletown Road
Parkton, MD 21120
(410) 357-5767

Bowley's Bait & Tackle Inc.
2917 Eastern Boulevard
Middle River, MD 21220
(410) 687-2107

Breezy Point Fishing Center
5230 Breezy Point Road
Chesapeake Beach, MD 20732
(410) 414-3558

Brunswick Hardware
302 West Potomac Street
Brunswick, MD 21716
(301) 834-9207

Chesapeake Bait and Tackle
344 Ritchie Highway
Severna Park, MD 21146
(410) 544-2248

Cheverly Sport Fair
5621 Landover Road
Hyattsville, MD 20784
(301) 277-8145

Clark's Bait & Tackle
3724 South Hanover Street
Brooklyn, MD 21225
(410) 355-4190

Clyde's Sport Shop
2307 Hammonds Ferry Road
Halethorpe, MD 21227
(410) 242-6108

Conowingo Fishing Center
2507 Shures Landing Road
Darlington, MD 21034
(410) 457-4609

Edgeworks Online
141 North Market Street
Frederick, MD 21701
(888) 520-0321
www.edgeworks-online.com

Extreme Bait & Tackle
1353 Old Post Road
Havre de Grace, MD 21078
(410) 942-0700

FBN Fly Shop
12081-A Tech Road
Silver Spring, MD 20904
(301) 622-4386 or (301) 622-3090
FBNTrout@aol.com

Fearl's Bait & Tackle
7002 North Point Road
Sparrows Point, MD 21219
(410) 388-0180

Fishbones Bait & Tackle
4729 Mountain Road
Pasadena, MD 21122
(410) 360-0573

Fisherman's Edge
1719½ Edmondson Avenue
Catonsville, MD 21228
(410) 719-7999

Fishing Island
8796 Sacramento Drive
Alexandria, VA 22309
(703) 780-8087

The Fishin Hole
7819 Wise Avenue
Dundalk, MD 21222
(410) 288-5070

Fletcher's Boat House
4940 Canal Road NW
Washington, DC 20007
(202) 244-0461

Fly Emporium of Baltimore
8600 Foundry Street
Savage, MD 20763
(410) 792-0340

Fox's Sport & Bait Shop
501 South Market Street
Frederick, MD 21701
(301) 663-3697

Galyan's
2 Grand Corner Avenue
Gaithersburg, MD 20878
(301) 947-0200

Gentleman Hunter Inc.
4829 Fairmont Avenue
Bethesda, MD 20814
(301) 907-4668

Herb's Tackle Shop
303 South Main Street
North East, MD 21901
(410) 287-5490

Holiday Sports
4520 Saint Barnabas Road
Temple Hills, MD 20748
(301) 894-3322
www.holidaysportsinc.com

JRS Fishing Tackle Outlet
8461 Fort Smallwood Road
Pasadena, MD 21122
(410) 439-2212

Keystone Sporting Goods Inc.
13611 Pennsylvania Avenue
Hagerstown, MD 21742
(301) 733-0373

Marty's Sporting Goods
95 Mayo Road
Edgewater, MD 21037
(410) 956-2238

Mike's Bait & Tackle
9766 Lee Highway
Fairfax, VA 22031
(703) 273-1436

Mike's Wholesale Bait Co.
801 Brandy Farm Lane
Gambrills, MD 21054
(410) 798-1755

Moeller's Bait & Tackle
Junction of RR 5 and RR 6
Charlotte Hall, MD 20622
(301) 884-3291

New Market Texaco
Maryland Highway 1, Box 1
Charlotte Hall, MD 20622
(301) 884-3291

Old Reisterstown Bait & Tackle
16 Westminster Road
Reisterstown, MD 21136
(410) 526-6500

Outdoor Sportsman Inc.
807 Eastern Boulevard
Essex, MD 21221
(410) 391-0222

Penn's Beach Marina
Foot of Lewis Street
Havre de Grace, MD 21078
(410) 939-2060

Reels & Wheels
17328 Taylors Landing Road
Sharpsburg, MD 21782
(301) 432-7281

Rick's Marine
11762 Point Lookout Road
Scotland, MD 20687
(301) 872-5156

Rod & Reel Dock
Maryland Highway 261
4165 Mears Avenue
Chesapeake Beach, MD 20732
(410) 257-2735

S & S Bait & Tackle
1710 Eastern Avenue
Baltimore, MD 21231
(410) 563-3243

Sarge's Market
751 Augustine Herman Highway
Elkton, MD 21921
(410) 398-9758

Scheible's Fishing Center
23 Wynne Road
Ridge, MD 20680
(301) 872-5185

Sets Sport Shop
509 York Road
Towson, MD 21204
(410) 823-1367

Shepherd Bait & Tackle
2007 Mount Vernon Avenue
Alexandria, VA 22301
(703) 684-0232

Sports Authority
595 East Ordnance Road
Glen Burnie, MD 21060
(410) 761-1151

Sports Authority
6250 Greenbelt Road
Greenbelt, MD 20770
(301) 220-4120

Stemple Bros. Bait & Tackle
51 Melitota Drive
Rising Sun, MD 21911
(410) 378-5594

The Tackle Box
22035 Three Notch Road
Lexington Park, MD 20653
(410) 863-8151

The Tackle Shop
1039 Frenchtown Road
Perryville, MD 21903
(410) 642-9166
goldmine49@aol.com

Tochterman and Sons Fishing Tackle
1925 Eastern Avenue
Baltimore, MD 21231
(410) 327-6942

Towsend Rock Run Landing
Rock Run Landing
P.O. Box 175
Port Deposit, MD 21904
(410) 378-3193

Tyler's Tackle Shop
8210 Bayside Avenue
Chesapeake Beach, MD 20732
(410) 257-6610

Warren's Bait Box
7403 Baltimore-Annapolis Boulevard
Glen Burnie, MD 21061
(410) 768-6977

Southern Maryland

Anglers Sport Center Limited
1456 Whitehall Road
Annapolis, MD 21401
(410) 974-4013

Bay Pro Shop
2855 Chesapeake Beach Road
Dunkirk, MD 20754
(301) 855-0351

Bayside Tackle
410 Severn Avenue
Annapolis, MD 21403
(410) 268-0660

Breezy Point Marina and Fishing
    Center
5230 Breezy Point Road
Chesapeake Beach, MD 20732
(301) 855-9894 (information)
(410) 414-9292 (store)
www.chesapeake.net/breezypointmarina

Bunky's Bait and Tackle
14448 Solomons Island Road South
Solomons, MD 20688
(410) 326-3241

Clyde's Sport Shop
2307 Hammonds Ferry Road
Halethorpe, MD 21227
(410) 242-6108

FBN Fly Shop
12081-A Tech Road
Silver Spring, MD 20904
(301) 622-4386 or (301) 622-3090
FBNTrout@aol.com

Fisherman's Edge
1719½ Edmondson Avenue
Catonsville, MD 21228
(410) 719-7999

Fort Washington Marina
13600 King Charles Terrace
Fort Washington, MD 20744
(301) 292-6455
http://mddnr.chesapeakebay.net/fish/
    rampquery.cfm?Facility=PG005

Fred's Sport Center
2895 Crain Highway
Waldorf, MD 20601
(301) 843-3040

Happy Harbor Inn
533 Deale Road
Deale, MD 20751
(410) 867-0949

Holiday Sports
4520 St. Barnabas Road
Temple Hills, MD 20748
(301) 894-3322
www.holidaysportsinc.com

JJ's Tackle Shop, Inc.
485 Deale Road
Deale, MD 20751
(410) 867-4515
www.jjstackle.com

Marty's Sporting Goods
95 Mayo Road
P.O. Box 116
Edgewater, MD 21037
(410) 956-2238

New Market Texaco
Maryland Highway 1, Box 1
Charlotte Hall, MD 20622
(301) 884-3291

Rick's Marine
11762 Point Lookout Road
Scotland, MD 20687
(301) 872-5156

Rod & Reel Dock
Maryland Highway 261
4165 Mears Avenue
Chesapeake Beach, MD 20732
(410) 257-2735

Scheible's Fishing Center
23 Wynne Road
Ridge, MD 20680
(301) 872-5185

Sports Authority
6250 Greenbelt Road
Greenbelt, MD 20770
(301) 220-4120

The Tackle Box
22035 Three Notch Road
Lexington Park, MD 20653
(410) 863-8151

Tyler's Tackle Shop
8210 Bayside Avenue
P.O. Box 434
Chesapeake Beach, MD 20732
(410) 257-6610

Warren's Bait Box
7403 Baltimore-Annapolis Boulevard
Glen Burnie, MD 21061
(410) 768-6977

Eastern Shore of Maryland

Ace Hardware
6807 Coastal Highway
Ocean City, MD 21842
(410) 524-2300

Anglers Sport Center
1456 Whitehall Road
Annapolis, MD 21401
(410) 974-4013

Bahia Marina Inc.
2107 Herring Way
Ocean City, MD 21842
(410) 289-7438
www.bahiamarina.com

Champion Tackle
3497 Snow Hill Road
Salisbury, MD 21804
(410) 548-2522

Chester River Marine Services
7501 Church Hill Road
Chestertown, MD 21620
(410) 778-2240

Choptank River Fishing Pier,
   Bait & Tackle
29761 Boling Broke Point, #D
Trappe, MD 21673
(410) 476-5785

Crisfield Bait & Tackle
326 Broadway
Crisfield, MD 21817
(410) 968-9440

Cypress Creek Archery &
   Sporting Goods
32719 Cypress Road
Millington, MD 21651
(410) 928-3871

Dave's Sport Shop
23701 Nanticoke Road
Quantico, MD 21856
(410) 742-2454

Herb's Tackle Shop
303 South Main Street
North East, MD 21901
(410) 287-5490

Hurlock Bait and Tackle
109 South Main Street
Hurlock, MD 21643
(410) 943-1600

Island Fishing & Hunting
115 South Piney Creek Road
Chester, MD 21619
(410) 643-4224
www.ifh.baweb.com

Millington Hardware
403 Cypress Street
Millington, MD 21651
(410) 928-3118

Ocean City Fishing Center
12940 Inlet Isle Lane
Ocean City, MD 21842
(410) 213-1121 or (800) 322-3065
www.ocfishing.com

Oyster Bay Tackle
Oyster Bay Shoppes
116th Street and Jamestown Road
Ocean City, MD 21842
(410) 524-3433
www.oysterbaytackle.com

Sassafras Harbor Marina
2 George Street
Georgetown, MD 21930
(410) 275-1144
www.sassafrasharbormarina.com

Sea Hawk Sport Center
643 Ocean Highway
Pocomoke City, MD 21851
(410) 957-0198
www.seahawksports.com

Shore Sportsman
8232 Ocean Gateway
Easton, MD 21601
(410) 820-5599

Skip's Bait and Tackle
210 Talbot Street
Ocean City, MD 21842
(410) 289-8555
www.oceancityfishing.com

Towsend Rock Run Landing
Rock Run Landing
P.O. Box 175
Port Deposit, MD 21904
(410) 378-3193

Vonnie's Sporting Goods
12503 Augustine Herman Highway
Kennedyville, MD 21645
(410) 778-5655

Winchester Creek Outfitters
313 Winchester Creek Road
Grasonville, MD 21638
(410) 827-7000

Delaware

A & K Enterprises
201 North Central Avenue
Laurel, DE 19956
(302) 875-5513

Bill's Sport Shop
1566 Highway 1
Lewes, DE 19958
(302) 645-7654
www.billssportshop.com

CAPT Bones Bait Tackle & Hunting
RR 13
Odessa, DE 19730
(302) 378-3377

Champion Tackle
3497 Snow Hill Road
Salisbury, MD 21804
(410) 548-2522

Dave's Sport Shop
23701 Nanticoke Road
Quantico, MD 21856
(410) 742-2454

Dick's Sporting Goods
Christiana Mall
Newark, DE 19711
(302) 738-8322

Donovan's Dock
42 Murderkill Avenue
Frederica, DE 19946
(302) 335-3500

Eastern Marine
931 South Chapel Street
Newark, DE 19713
(302) 737-6603

John E. Gechter Tackle & Bait
105 Cooper Avenue
Frederica, DE 19946
(302) 335-4885

Hook, Line & Sinker Fishing Center
Cape Henlopen State Park, DE 19958
(302) 644-2291

Indian River Marina
39415 Inlet Road
Rehoboth Beach, DE 19971
(302) 227-3071

Lewes Harbor Marina Bait & Tackle
217 Anglers Road
Lewes, DE 19958
(302) 645-6227

Ocean Pro Outfitters
2461 South Dupont Boulevard
Smyrna, DE 19977
(302) 653-2577

Old Hookers Bait & Tackle Shop
Fisherman's Wharf
105 Anglers Road
Lewes, DE 19958
(302) 645-8866

Slicer L C Sporting Goods
4101 Old Capitol Trail
Wilmington, DE 19808
(302) 836-6430

Smith's Bait Shop
500 Denny Street
Dover, DE 19901
(302) 744-9140

Taylored Tackle Shop
Road #2, Box 115
Seaford, DE 19973
(302) 629-9017
taylored@bwave.com

Guide Services and Head and Charter Boats

Western Maryland

Eastern Trophies Fly Fishing
6177 Tag Court
Woodbridge, VA 22193
(571) 213-2570
www.easterntrophies.com

Mark Kovach Fishing Services
406 Pershing Drive
Silver Spring, MD 20910-4253
(301) 588-8742
www.mkfs.com

Ken Penrod's Life Outdoors Unlimited
(301) 937-0010
www.penrodsguides.com

Playing Hookie Guide Service
635 North Vermont Street, #2
Arlington, VA 22203
(703) 243-5389
www.fishinginvirginia.net

Potomac Guide Service
(301) 582-9404
www.potomacguides.com

S&K Guide Service
509 Brandywine Boulevard
Wilmington, DE 19809-2955
(302) 545-9634 or (302) 764-1788
www.skguideservice.com

Northeastern Maryland

Backwater Angler
538 Monkton Road
Monkton, MD 21111
(410) 329-6821
www.dnr.state.md.us/outdoor
   adventures/onthefly.html

Bunky's Charter Boats
14448 Solomons Island Road South
P.O. Box 370
Solomons, MD 20688
(410) 326-3241

Karl's Bassin' Adventures Guide Service
(410) 272-6940 or (410) 459-7445
kwhbunch@comcast
www.karlsbassinadventures.com

Twilight Zone Charters
113 North Union Avenue
Havre de Grace, MD 21078
(410) 939-2948
rsborno@msn.com
www.tzcharters.com

Southern Maryland

Bay Paddlers
4055 Gorden Stinnett Avenue
P.O. Box 117
Chesapeake Beach, MD 20732
(410) 286-3663 or (301) 523-5284
www.baypaddlers.com

Bunky's Charter Boats
14448 Solomons Island Road South
P.O. Box 370
Solomons, MD 20688
(410) 326-3241

Captain Glenn A. James
8405 Bayside Road
Chesapeake Beach, MD 20732
(410) 286-8990 or (800) 322-4039
GJamesCapt@aol.com

Chesapeake Beach Fishing Charters
P.O. Box 757
Chesapeake Beach, MD 20732
(866) 532-9246 or (301) 855-4665
Deale charter boats:

Bay Lady, Captain Richard Grimes Sr.,
    (301) 261-5995 or (301) 529-1390

Bounty, (703) 938-1420, (703) 606-2669,
    or (410) 257-9315

Foolish Pleasure, Captain Tom Hea
    cock, (410) 257-2888 (home) or 410-
    804-8511 (boat), foolsplsur@aol.com

Fowl Play, Captain Rick Blackwell,
    (301) 812-0828 or (410) 218-9120
    (cell phone)

Happy Hour Charters, (301) 261-9580

Miss Grace, Captain Bob Baker, (410)
    320-6434, CaptainBob@MissGrace
    Charters.com

Natural Charters, (800) 519-1002

Reel Deale, Captain Michael Louis
    Garrett, (410) 867-4022 or (443) 336-
    4895 (cell phone)

Valerie Ann, Captain Ralph Barnes,
    (410) 231-2749

Additional Deale charter boat information can be found at www.dealecaptains
.com.

Dockoar and Tamshell Charters
7509 I Street
Chesapeake Beach, MD 20732
(301) 855-0739 (home) or (410)
    610-7420 (cell phone)
www.dockoar.com

Fishing C's Charters
2709 Placid Avenue
Parkville, MD 21234
(410) 668-0088

Miss Meagan Fishing Charters
1680 Heather Lane
Huntingtown, MD 20639
(410) 414-9662
www.missmeagan.com

Proud Mary Charters
1800 Wilson Road
Huntingtown, MD 20639
(410) 257-7363
www.proudmarycharters.com

Rod-N-Reel Charter Captains
4160 Mears Avenue
P.O. Box 99
Chesapeake Beach, MD 20732
(301) 855-8450 or (800) 233-2080
www.rodnreelinc.com

Solomons charter boats:

Barbie Doll, Captain Bob Adelman,
    (410) 798-5133,
    rfadelman@co.pg.md.us

Jennifer Ann, Captain Loch Weems,
    (410) 414-2459, lochjaws@netzero
    .com, www.jenniferanncharters.com

Lady Carole, Captain Brian Easter,
    (301) 884-4826, ladycarolecharters
    @yahoo.com, www.ladycarole
    charters.com

Margie D, Captain Margie Dove, (410)
    326-4151, margied@chesapeake.net

Rodbender, Captain Keith Allston,
    (301) 884-7139, camydor@yahoo
    .com, www.rodbendermd.com

Someday, Captain Gale Willett, (301) 645-5914, g.willett@att.net

Strike Zone, Captain Wally Williams, (410) 326-3345, captainwally@fish strikezone.com, www.fishstrikezone .com

Taurus, Captain Steve Barko, (410) 326-0444, sbarko@chesapeake .net, www.luckystrikefishingcharters .com

Teachers Pet, Captain Brian Elder, (410) 326-6254, captain@teacherspet-fishing.com, www.teacherspet-fishing .com

For a complete list of Solomons charter boats, go to www.fishsolomons.com/ pages/members.htm.

Eastern Shore of Maryland

Barbara Ann II and *Barbara Ann III* Charter Boat and Head Boat
Crisfield, MD
(410) 957-2562

Buck Fever Fishing Charter
20968 Bayside Avenue
Rock Hall, MD 21661
(410) 639-7507

Captain Greg Jetton
6944 Rock Hall Avenue
Rock Hall, MD 21661
(410) 639-7127

Captain Keith Ward
P.O. Box 246
Crisfield, MD 21817
(800) 791-1470

Captain Phil Hague
5146 Crosby Road
Rock Hall, MD 21661
(410) 639-9001

Captain Richard Manley
4798 Piney Neck Road
Rock Hall, MD 21661
(410) 639-7420

Captain Rob Hunter Jr.
25155 Chestertown Road
Chestertown, MD 21620
(410) 778-4941 or (443) 386-0882

Crisfield Charters
407 Franklin Avenue
Salisbury, MD 21804
(888) 584-9909
jmboat@intercom.net

Double A Charter Fishing
6311 Suicide Bridge Road
Hurlock, MD 21643
(410) 943-1124

Fish Fear Us Charters
21130 Carter Avenue
Rock Hall, MD 21661
(410) 639-7063

Fish Magnet
1439 Hoopers Island Road
Church Creek, MD 21622
(410) 397-3122

Fish N' Party II Charters
7824 Country Club Lane
Chestertown, MD 21620
(410) 708-6018

Wayne Gatling Guide Service
5889 Main Street
Rock Hall, MD 21661
(410) 778-3191

Gunsmoke Charters
6944 Rock Hall Road
Rock Hall, MD 21661
(410) 708-3825

Karns Charter and Yacht Service
124 Manor Avenue
Chestertown, MD 21620
(410) 708-2928

Leisure Charters
119 Fox Field Lane
Millington, MD 21651
(443) 480-2937

Misty Charters
5920 North Hawthorne Avenue
Rock Hall, MD 21661
(410) 639-7928

Morning Star, Captain Monty Hawkins
Ocean City Fishing Center
13001 Shantytown Road
Ocean City, MD 21842
(410) 520-2076
www.morningstarfishing.com

Ocean Princess
Old Towne Marina
Dorchester Street and the Bay
Ocean City, MD 21842
(410) 289 6226
http://theoceanprincess.com

Sassy Lady Charters
2513 Old House Point
Fishing Creek, MD 21634
(410) 397-3578

Sawyer Charters
1345 Hoopers Island Road
Church Creek, MD 21622
(410) 397-3743

Sportfishing Charters/Joint Venture
311 Nathan Avenue
Cambridge, MD 21613
(410) 228-7837

Sportfishing Charters/Miss Pritch
Taylor's Island Marina
931 Parsons Drive
Madison, MD 21648
(410) 901-2172

Steppin' Stone Charters
Crisfield and Wenona, MD
(410) 651-0121 (days)
(410) 651-5311 (nights)
tandsmarine@verizon.net

Stoney Cove Charters
5429 Stoney Ridge Road
Cambridge, MD 21613
(410) 228-8643

Striker Charters
3287 Golden Hill Road
Church Creek, MD 21622
(410) 397-3234
fishing@gootees.com

Tide Runner Fishing Charter
Hoopers Island, MD 21634
(410) 397-FISH

Delaware

AJ Sportfishing
807 Greenwood Road
Wilmington, DE 19807
(302) 684-3302 or (302) 540-7485
   (cell phone)
www.ajsportfishing.com

Amethyst, Captain Paul Henninger
P.O. Box 550
Millsboro, DE 19966
(302) 934-8119

Anglers Fishing Center
End of Anglers Road
Lewes, DE
(302) 644-4533

Fisherman's Wharf
Savannah Road, by the drawbridge
Lewes, DE
(302) 645-8862

Lil' Angler II (Anglers of Lewes, Inc.)
Lewes Harbor Marina, Anglers Road
Lewes, DE
(302) 645-8688

#1 Hooker Sportfishing
32240 Falling Point Road
Dagsboro, DE 19939
(302) 732-1274 or (717) 471-8502
   (cell phone)
hooker@atbeach.com

On Delivery
800 Miner Road
Crownsville, MD 21032
(443) 463-7849
ondeliveryspf@aol.com

Tranquila Sport Fishing
Slip #17, Lewes Harbor Marina
Lewes, DE 19958
(302) 745-1503

Index

About the Authors

Ruta Vaskys and Martin Freed have had a number of careers, including faculty appointments at various colleges, entrepreneurs, trapping and collecting wild herbs in Vermont and Alaska, and outdoors and conservation writers and photographers.

Ruta has a BS in occupational therapy and a master's in counseling. She has worked in both fields and has been a professional commercial artist. She studied at the Maryland Institute of Art and the Richmond Professional Institute and did her graduate studies at the University of Alaska, Fairbanks.

Martin taught geology, chemistry, oceanography, and mathematics at a number of colleges and universities. He graduated from Coastal Carolina with a BS and did his graduate work at the University of Alaska in physical oceanography.

Before going to graduate school, the couple built a cabin in the Green Mountains of Vermont and lived without electricity or running water for a number of years. After graduate school, Martin and Ruta made Alaska their home. In 1988 they bought another home on the Eastern Shore of Virginia and currently split the year between the two states.

Ruta and Martin started writing about the outdoors in the mid-1980s and have had articles published in many regional as well as national publications, including *Fur, Fish and Game, Easy Street*, the *Eastern Shore News*, the *Mid-Atlantic Fisherman, What's Up Annapolis, Shotgun Magazine*, the *Chesapeake Angler*, the *Salisbury Times, Alaska, Fish Alaska*, and *Game and Fish*. Both are members of the Outdoor Writers Association of America (OWAA). The couple's first book, *Fishing Virginia*, was published by The Lyons Press in 2007.

Ruta and Martin met on top of Mount Abraham in Vermont in 1976 and have been climbing mountains together ever since.